THE SPARKLING-EYED BOY

The
Sparkling-Eyed Boy

A Memoir of Love,
Grown Up

Amy Benson

A MARINER ORIGINAL
HOUGHTON MIFFLIN COMPANY
BOSTON · NEW YORK
2004

For information about permission to reproduce selections
from this book, write to Permissions, Houghton Mifflin Company,
215 Park Avenue South, New York, New York 10003.

Visit our Web site: www.houghtonmifflinbooks.com.

ISBN-13: 978-0-618-43321-6
ISBN-10: 0-618-43321-X

Library of Congress Cataloging-in-Publication data is available.

Book design by Melissa Lotfy

Printed in the United States of America

MP 10 9 8 7 6 5 4 3 2 1

Portions of this book have appeared in *Connecticut Review,*
River Styx, Literal Latte, Quarterly West, Climate Control,
Fourth Genre, Sonora Review, River Teeth,
New Orleans Review, and *Skidrow Penthouse.*

For my mother, for her generous and tenacious spirit;
for Nancy, for her fierce brain and dear heart;
and for Douglas, with whom, now, all stories begin and end.

Author's Note

This book takes as its ground a place monumentally important to me as a child and a person who became for me a symbol of that place — of the best, and most difficult, things about it. Though we were close as teenagers, I have seen him only briefly a few times since then and do not know who he is as an adult. Any conjecture about his present self is simply my attempt to try on different continuities between past and present, familiarity and an exile of sorts; just as the fictional chapters in this book are attempts to imagine the great distance now between us diminishing. Neither of these things is possible, however. The past does not collapse into the present, and the distance remains. Just as it should.

Contents

❧

PART IV: OUR LIVES — WITH A LEAD AND
A HOOK AND A CLOSE

❧

PART II, REPRISED: IF IT WERE TO HAPPEN,
IT MIGHT HAPPEN LIKE THIS

❧

PART V: THE FINAL DAYS OF ROMANTICISM

Thanks

I would like to thank the people who have supported me in many and varied ways while I wrote this book. Thanks to Douglas; thanks to my family—Richard, Patsy, Janet, and Eden, and the Repettos; thanks to my friends who critiqued and encouraged—Catie, Lisa, Susan, Nancy, and Dennis; thanks to Kerry Klett; thanks to my former students and colleagues at Northwest Missouri State University; thanks to the teachers who have changed me: Robin Behn, Donald Callen, Elizabeth Meese, Darius Ogloza, Thomas Rabbitt, and Richard Rand; thanks to the people who very tangibly have made this possible —Ted Conover, Michael Collier, the Katharine Bakeless Nason Prize, Bill Clegg, and the team at Houghton Mifflin, most importantly Deanne Urmy, Melissa Grella, Corrina Lesser, and Alison Kerr Miller; and, finally, thanks to the people I knew in the Upper Peninsula for sharing their home.

INTRODUCTION

To the famous list of three events that anthropologists say characterize human life around the globe — birth, marriage, and death — I wonder if it isn't time to add a fourth: first love.

Who among us has not had a sparkling-eyed boy or girl — that person we met when young and couldn't keep our minds off, the one we hungrily wanted to look at again and again and again? And have never forgotten?

Most crushes are probably ephemeral, and the power they exert can make them seem silly, a childish example of emotion trumping reason. *"Amour fou,"* say the French; or "puppy love" (a phrase I have always hated for its dismissiveness, for who loves more passionately than the young?). Others, however, are clearly deep and last a long time. And profundity lurks in something that focuses all our attention and touches us to the core.

Those who have held a crush know that it can be hard to make other people understand. But here in your hands is something new. Amy Benson's book makes infatuation fascinating to *us*. I have never read anything like it; in the intensity of its feeling and the sheer music of its language, it leapt at me from the stack of submissions for this year's Bakeless Prize in Creative Nonfiction.

Benson has written a singular, mostly one-sided love story.

Like most good fiction, it is a product much more of the writer's mind than of the give and take between actual lovers. But the sparkling-eyed boy, a real person, never seems to me misrepresented or exploited; Benson is too smart to broadly objectify him. If we do not know his mind, that does not mean he is belittled by her adoration.

In fact, as Benson notes ruefully, in the beginning it was *he* who had the crush on *her*. Only later do the roles reverse, and we see how, over time, this prolonged, distanced relationship has had agony and loneliness, crossed signals and mixed messages and bad timing, just like a more conventional one.

The book is also a searing self-examination, the literary diary of a woman who follows herself and the boy from the weirdly pure impulse that first love represents to a child or adolescent to the more complicated thing it implies for a woman headed toward thirty. Her thoughts of the sparkling-eyed boy distract her from other relationships but bind her to a youth she cherishes. She recognizes how unrealistic her feelings are, knows that she is probably idealizing the now-grown "boy," but is not prepared to admit that this is necessarily bad. He is, she writes, "the perfect elsewhere on which I might dwell." Upset at not seeing him one night, she is told by a wise friend, "You're pining for *something;* you're not really pining for *him.*" I believe Amy Benson's daring self-exposure in matters of the heart will resonate with many readers.

This volume is also just a sheer pleasure to read. As they hear her story, I think readers will be enmeshed, as I was, by Benson's remarkable dexterity with language, by the careful crafting and inspiration that result in verbal surprises on practically every page. There is music here, and poetry, and they combine with Benson's recursive examinations of self to move the art of memoir in a fascinating and promising new direction.

Maybe one other reason I loved this book is that I had a crush on a pretty tomboy from kindergarten to about sixth grade; she was, after my mom, the first love of my life. She was the only one who could keep up with me — even beat me — at playground sprints and spelling tests. We shared captainship of the safety patrol. She was brave and strong, once whipping a neighborhood braggart in a fight, a feat I wildly admired. We were terribly shy; I don't think we ever even held hands or did much more than walk home together after school. But for years after we fell out of touch I would think of her, wonder what she was doing, and occasionally torture myself by contemplating what our lives might have been like if we had declared our love and stayed with that first, pure thing.

Then, quite a long time after, I was spared further second-guessing of the choices I had made when I heard from a mutual acquaintance that my first love had lived with the same person now for years and years — and that this life partner was a woman. It would never have worked anyway. With a stroke came closure; but how many of us are so lucky?

Ted Conover
NEW YORK CITY

PART I

In Medias Res

Up North

They called us trolls because we lived for nine months of the year below (that is, south of) the bridge. The Mackinac Bridge connects the Upper Peninsula of Michigan with the Lower Peninsula. For the five miles of the bridge, all you see is water and sky, blurring out at the edges. People died erecting its towers and suspending its cables over water three hundred feet deep — they say the body of at least one man is trapped in a concrete tower. In high winds, tiny un-American cars like mine have been blown off the bridge, down to the storm-blackened Straits of Mackinac. I imagine the impact every time — flying free from the car, the beautiful water like an anvil driving the bones in my toes all the way up into my soft neck.

Some people who live far from the Great Lakes don't know that Michigan comes in two pieces disconnected by water. The Lower Peninsula looks like a mitten, a comfort to trolls far away from home, who can always, when asked by strangers where they're from, raise their right hands — palm forward and lined like a road map, thumb out to the side — and point to their hometown. But the mitt of Michigan is not charming to the billy goats above the bridge. Yoopers, as they often call themselves (a phonetic version of UPers), are surrounded on every side by the largest quantity of fresh water on the globe;

they're flooded with evergreens and wild animals and independence. Even though they're attached by land to Wisconsin, Michigan's downstate capital, Lansing, rules them. Detroit, in turn, through its sheer size and auto industry clout, rules Lansing, and yoopers hate Detroit in every way. That's where we're from, 350 miles to the south.

The yooper boys I knew told my sister and me they felt sorry for us, all the secret ways the city must be ruining us: to live where things are assembled, and the noise, the grease and sweat that must work its way into our skin. And the stench of the Three Sisters smokestacks, and the Rouge River, the Detroit River, none of which they'd seen — but they could imagine the scent of things burning that never should have been things in the first place. And the blacks. The blacks, with their hot crack pipes and babies and guns that were not at all like their own guns. To accept concrete and traffic and crime and the constant hazy glow that unravels the significance of stars; to live by deforming, more and more every day, what we had been given, down to the compacted dirt under our feet — how could we stand it?

They said all of these things in ugly or touching or frightened or silent ways. And I for one believed in places that didn't looked humbled by humans, where more things grew than were produced, where I could thrill myself for whole moments at a time that I was the last person on earth. I believed those boys were right and I was, by some misfortune, a troll.

Most of us downstaters get as far north as Mackinac Island: we take a hydroplane ferry across the Straits of Mackinac, eat fudge, swoon around the Grand Hotel, pretending we have erased crass modernity but secretly complaining that the island doesn't allow cars.

Those who actually cross the bridge find that the U.P. is at least ten times as big as Rhode Island and has only one area code for its sparse population. The seven-month winters and towns of thirty or forty people drive off the weak and the ambitious. The U.P. might as well be Alaska—ours only because we're greedy. And, as Alaska was for its gold, the U.P. was prospected for timber and shipping routes almost two centuries ago by the shy, the sturdy, the malignant, and the insane. But this is just the history of America, distilled.

Some people press on past the bridge, though. A handful of downstaters, like my family, perch nervously in their subdivisions most of the year, waiting to snap alive in the U.P. for a few summer months. My suburban family heated our house with a wood stove, cut and split the wood, raised and canned the year's vegetables, made our own clothes; in short, we did everything we could to live in a time when living required more effort. So when we packed the car up tight each June and drove north, it was understood we were going home. Of course, we noticed the satellite dishes, the Schlitz, the propped-up cars in the U.P.; and, frankly, we needed them in order to claim we liked the wilderness and its rough love better than the yoopers did. A favorite sentiment of my parents' as we'd watch a pink sun drown itself in Lake Huron, our bathing suits still wet, sand in the seashell curves of our ears, quiet everywhere except for the rhythmic wash of the waves and our own breath, which were one: *Remember this when we're trapped in the middle of the crowded winter.*

Even though my sister and I wore hand-me-downs and homemade pants, we lived in Detroit and read *National Geographic,* we'd been to both coasts—we'd been to Europe, for god's sake. We never spoke of these things with our locals, though. We knew that what could give us power in Detroit, like Europe or hair spray, was a liability in the U.P.

We were "summers," people who spend their summers in the same vacation spot every year. Summers are displaced people: we learn not to be at home at home. But my sister and I knew enough to need a home, and so we wanted their home. We wanted to be more local than our locals. And we thought we had a way in: we could trace our family to founders of the minuscule town. The boys could see our grandfather's childhood home falling to bits at the base of the hill that sloped down to the bay. We were no mere "tourists."

Oh how my sister and I curled our lips against the tourists. They stayed in the handful of rental cabins just down the shore from us and pulled up with inboard boats behind too-shiny trucks. They came to fish and slap mosquitoes from their pale thighs. They stayed for a week or two, thought it was pretty, wrinkled their noses at the sulfury well water and said how the fishing wasn't as good as last year. They *used* this place, but they didn't *need* it, and it didn't dictate to them what was both beautiful and true for the rest of their lives.

All summer we swam with our locals, ate Zingers and sometimes venison steak with them, looked through their yearbooks with them, fell through the rotten boards of their tree houses with them, got summer jobs with them, drank in the woods with them, sometimes we kissed them, broke our hearts with them. And then, every September, we drove back south without them.

Come the next June, we needed them to circle us, sniff our hair, knock us down, and accept us back with them, as one of their own.

Let's face it: my sister and I were fresh meat to the local boys. Their charms had become stale to the local girls by the time we'd discovered one another. They recited every story they knew by heart in accents that made us giggle — *Oh yah? Tell me aboat it, eh?* They smiled at the charming miniatures of themselves in our rapt eyes.

When kids realize the end of their road is not the end of the world, they wonder if they could have fallen into a better place, a better spread of chromosomes. They are on the verge of a dissatisfied life, a grown-up life, the life of a summer.

Sure, the boys thought they might eventually get laid, but what they really wanted, what we *did* give up easily, was the sense that they had fallen, by the love of no flimsy god, into the best place on earth. Their wondering was over and their dazzled lives could begin.

He attached himself to me from the first; I don't know why. He didn't like makeup on girls and I wasn't allowed to wear it. I didn't know how to flirt. Maybe it was as simple as that. Whatever the reason, we stuck together, as friends, for years, while I abused his feelings, pining for another local who, in turn, abused my feelings. This is so typical. We were practicing for life: neglecting what you have and who you are for what you can't have, who you won't ever be.

But we never scorned where we were; we knew what beauty stitched itself into the shifting moods of the water and the serious pine trees crowding right down to the water's edge, daring us to walk among them. He loved with loyalty. He would never leave this place and be from somewhere else, struggling to breathe through vestigial gills. And, as I got ready to go to college, he knew before I did I could never stay.

He married someone else three years after I left and didn't return. I can only think he needed someone he'd still be touching when he was sixty, skin to skin in the middle of the night.

How do we make meaning out of what does not abide?

He lived, lives still, in a town of maybe forty people and a general store/restaurant/bar, post office, and Catholic church. I can't remember everything about him as well as I'd like, and I have no way of knowing what I've forgotten. A few pictures I have of him, though, tell me much of what I need to know.

They were taken during the town's centennial celebration in 1979 and published in a little book commemorating the festivities and the family history of the area. He was only nine or so (though I was there, in a homemade pioneer dress, we wouldn't meet for another three years), but he got his black-and-white photo in the booklet twice. In one, a fourth grade class photo, he's grinning and he has his arm around the boy next to him, about to pinch his cheek with a quick, sharp hand. In the other, my favorite, he is in a rocking contest, propped up in a large rocker. Cushions protect his bony frame, his knees meet in the middle, and his feet fly out to either side, like the hooves of a new colt. But I'm most interested in his face: he's pushing it toward the camera, a smile so tight across his freckled skin that his eyes are nearly pinched closed. This is a being capable of feeling joy through his whole body to the tips of his teeth. This boy is not mean, nor is he afraid. The centennial booklet belongs to my grandmother, and she keeps asking for it, but I make excuses, put her off. I can't give up that image of life.

I have another picture that might help to explain. It's a picture of me taken by the sparkling-eyed boy with my parents' camera. I've always liked the picture, probably because it's anomalous: I'm fifteen or sixteen, wearing my sister's clothes, and I look pretty and grown up, like a girl someone's going to marry. I was neither of those things, though, and I hadn't yet agreed to go out with him. I'm looking at him over my left shoulder, something unmistakable in my eyes — the knowledge of being loved. I wasn't sure what made me lovable to him; I was just grateful that, no matter how I tested him, he stuck around, always willing to show me his heart. This was a boy I could count on.

These stories are about permanence and temporality — two equally strong poles of human yearning. Death is tragic, we feel. The death of love, also tragic. Another birthday, a sinking helium balloon, the slow distortions of memory, tragedies all. Most of us need to think these things won't happen to us, so we make choices that might root us to our selves: we get religion, or get married, buy a house, have a kid. But our acquisitions only tell us how mortal we are, glued to one spot, embodying one self until we die.

But, on the other hand, if we have chosen nothing — rather, if we have chosen to hover always in a state of possibility, never committing to a place, a person, a job, an argument, an idea, how do we know who we are? What can we point to in order to account for ourselves? We will have left not even the slightest impression on the loose soil of the earth or the skins of the people on it. I will never experience what it's like to decide early on to stay and eventually die in the same place I was born, the deep knowing that might have been mine.

I admit I am terrified by sameness. The thought of not periodically changing my life is like an unpacked steamer trunk on my chest. But before the sparkling-eyed boy married, I had a wholly unfair expectation that he would be my permanence. That wherever I went, whatever choices I made or refused to make, he had chosen me permanently and kept some part of me safe and constant. I wanted to have every possible thing and to lose nothing in the process. Honestly, don't we all?

I miss him still. But he has become a soapstone in my pocket, shaped less like himself than the heart of my hand, wearing to the grip of my fingers, grooved with the lines of my palm.

A Primer on Rootlessness

When you leave the place you will only later call home, you become, rather suddenly, though you might not know it for quite some time,

like a fish without scales, the naked diamonds of its puckered skin flashing their ascent from the bottom to the air-choked top,

like a flock of birds with pebble-filled bones — though the stones themselves may be quite lovely, the birds will plummet toward the ground as if they had suddenly fallen in love with it. Once there, they will embrace it, wings wide and necks crooked in touchingly naive surprise,

like an eye leaking water, its strangely beautiful circles of color buckling. One crack, two cracks, and it is a flap of spent cells, no longer an eye,

like a moth flying more and more erratically, aiming for the obscene head of a flower and hitting the stem instead, an oval of its wing dust ground into the finger pad of a human,

· · ·

like two hands of fingers, nails extracted—they carry a sense of bereavement times ten and they cannot catch fine and shrinking things,

like a tiny country that can find itself on no map or atlas. It wonders, was it a dream? Those years of living and naming and fighting and crying. And the tales we tell of our headdresses and the ways we sing ourselves to sleep.

like a river damned, swelling like a goiter, watching its sickly abdomen trail out the other side, raging under the pressure of itself upon itself, wishing for a pin a tooth an awl a tiny hole an eyelash crack,

like a fish, scaled.

But the news is not all bad. Though you cannot rescale yourself, though you cannot go home, you may never know yourself better than when you are about to float, white on a dark streak of lake, breathing like a beast.

The Way It Goes When We Close Our Eyes

I have dreams about you. This is what I will tell the sparkling-eyed boy.

I instruct my students in Introduction to Literature: think of the last truly beautiful or frightening or shockingly real dream you had. If I'm lucky, their faces take on expression. Did you try to tell someone about it? How did that feel, the telling? I am trying to demonstrate something about the fear of solipsism in the work of Li Po or Wordsworth, or in *Hamlet*. It's frustrating, the students say, willing to talk about their *own* lives but not the lives in the books. Their friend, girlfriend, mother, didn't understand, couldn't really see what they had seen in their dreams, not really. But, I ask, have you ever stopped trying to tell? I ask, but don't ask, Aren't you spurred by the lonely echo in your chest?

I would say to him: *I dream that everything I need to know could come from your mouth.*

The dreams started a few years after his marriage — when I was twenty-three, twenty-four. I refuse to own them; they came to me like a haint. Once every few months for the first years I had these dreams, I would go to bed, filled with the forgettable detritus of the day, and he would seep into my sleep and trigger the same encounter over and over. Life would become ridiculously simple for however long it takes us to dream up the beginnings, middles, and ends of our sleeping stories.

The one I remember best, the one that told me I had a genuine pattern of dreams on my hands, begins on my family's dirt road. A group of people is gathered, but the sparkling-eyed boy and I are, essentially, alone with each other. The convergence of sky, tree, and water in this very spot implies that we'd be blind if we weren't looking at each other, as if this background and foreground couldn't exist separately. As if, in other words, we have been apart far too long.

"Hi," I say.

"Hi," he says.

In my dreams we are not brilliant or even believable conversationalists.

"Why did you leave me?" he asks. "You went to college and I didn't hear from you anymore. You left and you never came back."

"I know," I say. "I'm sorry. I guess I didn't think I could have a life up here. I thought there were other things I had to do. I guess I wanted to forget what I was so I could become someone different for a while."

"Yes," he says, as if he didn't even have to ask. "I've missed you," he says. His face is sad but certain, as if the end of this conversation is already determined and the words we choose must be said but can't alter the outcome. (My favorite kind of speech, the kind I can't fumble.) We have, both of us, been rehearsing with the same script for a long time.

I want to rush to the end. I say: "How could you have gotten married? And so soon! You were only twenty-one."

He says: "I'm sorry. I guess I panicked—I thought you'd never come back, and, maybe, up here, no one would ever marry me."

I nod at our mutual accusations, our mutual apologies, as if to say: Yes. We have been foolish. We have done what we needed to do. (This paradox goes unacknowledged.) But now we'll set things right.

"I'll have to find work up here," I say.

"I'll have to have a talk with my wife," he says.

We wander down to a secluded bend in the road. At this point in the summer, the grass at the side of the road is nearly taller than we are, and the smell of fresh mint is drifting up from the ditches. We step toward each other, the lengths of our bodies almost touching, conscious that someone might see us. This close, our pores open to each other and we breathe deeply, sending each other to our lungs, then on to every somal cell. For no reason at all he smells like lambs, cedar, and sunshine. Then we kiss, a kiss slower and deeper than any I've had. It's almost as if we are merely breathing into each other. Everything will be different from now on.

I dream we are so normal. Neither of us melts into a griffin or becomes the other's mother.

Of course, I wake up then; after all, what could possibly happen next? I am not an unhappy person, really. Melancholic, I'll allow, but not truly unhappy. However, I do wake every morning, my head buzzing with plans as to how I can avoid disappointing myself any further than I already have. On less cheerful days, I wake with the certain knowledge that today I will not be *able* to avoid disappointing even people I don't know. But on the mornings after these dreams, I wake deeply unconscious of my life, of the patterns of my brain, and of my true opinion of myself. I am alive only to love, only to the peace of being enveloped. It's like—yes, like what we pretend to re-member of the womb. Only it lasts a mere ten seconds or so. I wake fully and then I am again incomplete, as if I had been a conjoined twin, sharing a heart with my brother and now I am forced to limp along with two ventricles only, the blood never making it to my extremities. But (as only an addict would say), pale as I am, tepid as is my pulse, the ten seconds are worth it.

I dream in sunlight, great sheets of yellow, as if we could reach out our tongues and taste it and it would shrink from us like cotton candy.

Isn't it sometimes difficult to remember that dreams are not fortunes, and that fortunes, even those in the backs of scented magazines or folded into cookies, are not gifts of foresight? The sparkling-eyed-boy dreams were so shockingly sweet and necessary that for a while I refused to interpret them lest they stop coming. I wanted them to be visitations, predictions, psy-chic phenomena, and if I dissected them I would find them merely inanimate, in severed pieces.

I dream we are like water when it meets other water.

Here is another example, a later variation on the sparkling-eyed-boy dream: We are again on my family's property in the Upper Peninsula, only this time we're in my grandmother's cabin and we are wrapped up together in a tarp on the floor. We're not in any danger, but there is some suggestion of hav-ing been wrapped in the tarp by, say, a burglar or as a practical joke. If someone finds us like this, we have the excuse, at any rate, that, though we are exactly where we would like to be, we have not acted of our own volition to get there. We are having our usual dialogue about the choices we've made, but this is a very quiet dream and our low murmurs are indecipherable even to me, the dreamer. Sometimes he is on top, sometimes

I am, but we don't do anything; we don't do *it*. Our aspect is more like a loving couple *after* sex. On our first meeting in years, we can easily acquire a post-sex, defenseless melting without any of the acrobatics. (What I want—or at least what my subconscious wants—from the sparkling-eyed boy is not, apparently, sex.) Somehow, come morning, which we've watched break over the bay, we are freed from the tarp. In a dream leap, we are suddenly in the back seat of a car, being driven out of my family's property. The looks that we silently share assure us both that it's not over, it will never be over between us. Strangely, I think I am also the driver, catching these looks in the rearview mirror and comprehending what they mean, experiencing both the pleasure of secret love and the pleasure of discovering the secret.

Why does it afterward feel as if my brain has given me an unexpected gift and snatched it back again? The gift is almost always the same: the ability to talk after so long, to explain ourselves to each other; the unspeakable relief that we still love each other; the threat of discovery; and at the most a few kisses. No matter the configurations of my life—friends, boyfriends, graduate programs, jobs—he comes again.

I may be dreaming about an ability to break the stranglehold of the past, to escape the consequences of my choices. As I sleep, I am allowed to have fragmented my world and then find it whole again. I *am*, to push the metaphors, allowed to unring a bell. The sound waves, fat and satisfying, roll back to me as if I had called their names and they loved me.

Perhaps I am dreaming of a less complex world. The dreams allow me to exercise a taste for reversals—videotapes running backwards, systems becoming simpler, entropy undone. There is his self and my self and we know just what to say to each other, just what we will do from now on.

Maybe I'm just trying to experience that moment I will

never experience — knowing his present mind, letting him know mine. We could help each other understand the past; I know we could. We could be kind to each other, tell each other that in a disappointing world, we nevertheless would be wrong to doubt the endurance of love.

Some people say that a good way to understand dreams is to think of every person in them as you, or at least as some part of you. If this is true, I can understand the repeated variations on this dream as the reunion of two parts of myself: my present self, none too pleased with itself, meets up with my younger self, braver and more unified. We find out we have been sad without each other, that we have loved each other all along. Thus, I can feel, for a moment, some peace, some wholeness.

How terrifying, though, if even our subconscious can't imagine other people besides the self, if we are as isolated in our dream life as we are in our waking one. More than any-thing, I need to think of these dreams as love stories, a fulfill-ment of both our wishes. The sparkling-eyed boy started ap-pearing to me again, wholly unbidden, until I agreed to notice him, honor our losses — whatever they might have been — and mend them. That's really him, pressing my hand between both of his. Not me, him — freckled, intent, more serious than usual. Really. I never would have started writing this if I thought my brain could not fully imagine him, if every dream had been just me, multiplied.

I dream lately that you won't speak to me. My shoes are all wrong. And then I am cast, like a Copenhagen statue, gray and forever.

But have you ever stopped trying to tell someone about your dreams? make them understand you? I ask my students. Aren't you terrified by the solitude in your body cavity?

I have dreams about you. I have decided that this is what I will tell him if I press a note into his hand this summer when no one is looking and the note asks him to meet me at noon the next day or the day after that at the roadside park along the shore of Lake Huron and he comes and we look at one another and don't know what to say. We will shuffle and blush and I will know that I shouldn't have asked him and he shouldn't have come. Nevertheless, I will say, *I have dreams about you and I wake up deeply satisfied. So what are we going to do about that?*

The Art of Letter Writing

or, "Hey! It's been a long time!"

I remember standing on the gravel road in my green plaid bathing suit, my hair dripping dark spots in the dust, holding a note in my hand. The sparkling-eyed boy had just pressed this worried lump into my fourteen-year-old palm and gunned away on his four-wheeler. A handwritten letter is usually a triumph for a young girl: here, finally, an unambiguous gesture. But I felt the weight of obligation folded into a hard knot under my fingers and the gravel boring into the bare soles of my feet. In the palm of my hand were sentences like *When you danced with me last night at the Community Center, why were you not really dancing with me? Why don't you like me back? I've waited for you to like me for a long time.*

Years later I write a letter to the sparkling-eyed boy:
"... I'll bet you're surprised to hear from me! I can't believe it's been seven years! Can you? So much has happened. ... I hear that you got married a few years ago. Congratulations!!"
Would that I could wrap the exclamation points around my throat until I agreed to tell the truth about just one thing. Would it do, though, to turn all my secrets inside out so the thick skin is on the inside and the wet insides infect?

No, it would not. So I make it easy on him, writing a letter he will have no problem showing to his wife. I avoid even one "I remember," even one claim on the vast stretches of time over which she can cast no shadow. Still, I feel greediness churn up the back of my throat. I have no right to even the smallest scrap of him, and yet here is my carefully fingered horde.

I am convinced—if he loved me first, he loved me best. I spent only summers in his corner of the Upper Peninsula, but wasn't he waiting for me every June with a grin, his dimples integral flecks in my summer landscape? Weren't we always working side by side in the stuff of the earth—the strawberry patch, the gravel pit, the hay fields? Wasn't he strong enough to be always holding up his tenderest, most possessive heart in his rough hands, only to have me slap it down—"not now, not like that"?

I have proof: on my fourteenth birthday, he gave me a glowing wooden bowl he'd made with his own hands. A perfectly fitted lid opened with a slight popping sound to a picture of himself lying in the bottom, an unevenly cut school picture with sleepy eyes, hair cut straight across his forehead, one deviant tuft arching up, and two dimples boring straight through his cheeks to something good, unsure, and longing in the center of his brain. "Love, ——" was scratched on the back. Oh, didn't I blush and squirm? Honestly, I was a silly girl, the silliest, courting the approval of scornful boys, arrogant strangers, grownups, and anyone else who couldn't possibly matter. I didn't want to have to see the sparkling-eyed boy so always by my side. Yet there he was, planted in front of me, cowlick and all, demanding that I notice something real, like the work of his hands on the body of a tree, or the hands themselves, connected as they were to the rest of him.

But I had just become a weak adolescent and wasn't ready to give up the small powers adolescence affords: trying to level what I could, to build what I couldn't. I took the bowl home with me, though, at the end of the summer and set it on the dresser in my bedroom, a scrap of tree to comfort my separation from forest and lake. In a few moments of clarity now and then, I thought of how happy I would be if that bowl could make my heart glow like its own piney grain.

I wish I could say that the bowl moved with me once I left home for school, and that it followed me from state to state, a familiar, solid thing. I wish I could say the bowl is sitting next to my bed, filled with fortunes from cookies, coins from Greece and China, ticket stubs, river stones, and one comical school picture, but I don't even know where the bowl is, or the heart of the tree from which it was cut, or the heart of the boy who cut it.

"Do you and the rest of the gang ever find time to go swimming anymore?"

These towns of thirty or forty peaked a hundred years ago, when timber was the hottest thing going. And going and going until every tree not sawed off at the base had been knocked down in the rush to get timber down to the water and float it east or west through the Great Lakes. Pictures from this time are vivid—men grinning and sweating over two-person saws; eight, ten bucks strung up in a row, the snow dark on the ground below them; boys poking mounds of bounty-killed coyotes or wolves. And then the bounty was gone and there wasn't much left for anyone.

And yet when we were kids there, long after the crowds of loggers moved on and the pictures dimmed, our bodies in water felt momentous. We were all daring slivers of import, diving from the county dock into the deep, cold water. Too alive with gall, we were, too pleased with ourselves and the touch of the world on our skins not to matter. Surely that's worth remembering:

A dock and a fine summer's day in a string of fine summer's

days. Here is one with red hair, glasses, and baby fat diving off the high, rickety platform. He requires the very most attention and receives the least. Here is one, a golden boy, kind but cagey, adhering to a TV-cool that has somehow trickled into the wilderness. He's an alpha male in black swim trunks and sunglasses and is the first to know about AIDS and makes jokes about it, back when kids like him weren't going to get it. Here is his brother, devilish and dumb, with terrible curls and tube socks. He splashes, cannonballs, and smokes with a pure heart. Here is their cousin, the sparkling-eyed boy, skinny, freckled, occasionally punched, usually dancing just out of reach, his eyes flecked with jokes, venom, and pain. Here is a pretty girl, dark-haired and slender. She doesn't like getting very wet. She behaves as girls are supposed to, only more flirtatiously. She has suntan oil, a yellow bikini, and ready words. She punishes her sister with her grace. Here is her sister, sturdy in her green plaid bathing suit — almost her only summer attire. She is awkward and unconcerned, shamed and arrogant, permanently lake-bound. In her childish imagination, she thinks strength might be taken for beauty: if she swims out farther than anyone, if she is the last to come out of the water, she might become mysterious, otherworldly, special. But the only one who waits for her to climb out is the sparkling-eyed boy. He has followed her with his eyes all afternoon; she has followed the golden boy with hers; and the golden boy has looked nowhere in particular. They walk home together, waterlogged, lonely at the end of the day.

They have sullied the water with their needs. They apologize as the sun sets and begin again as it rises.

"I'm still in school. Can you believe that? You'd think I liked it or something."

I realize there is little I could say about my life now that would make any sense to him. For example, I laughed the first time I heard the word *reify*—come again? as in "*if* it all over again"? or "once more with the *if*"? Last week I used *reify* three times in as many paragraphs.

Going far away to school and not coming back for any more summers was clearly the end of my comprehensibility for the sparkling-eyed boy. And perhaps this is why I write the letter, to straighten out my tongue, iron the unwieldy bumps it has acquired. Is this really what I want, though? To dribble what I have accreted through my fingers, eyeing wistfully what someone else might want me to be? Here is a buttered tightrope: It won't do to imagine what I would actually do with the sparkling-eyed boy if I had him; what he would do with me.

"So I hear the construction business you started with —— —— is going well. My dad said you were even working on a few summer homes in —— last year."

I am fifteen and still frustrating his advances when we drive with his best friend and my father deep into the northern Ontario wilderness. We are going for a week to the Esnagami fishing camp perched on a hundred deep and winding lakes. The boys have saved all year for this trip and my dad is paying my way. We drive past town and store, reservation and road, beyond the reach of irony and of plumbing, until only a seaplane can take us farther. In little aluminum boats we have our arms, the pole, and nylon line to bring the lake's most concentrated twists of life struggling to the surface. Proud fisher-girl among men. We carry, we cast, we portage, we cook and eat fish over brand-new fires.

But one evening the sparkling-eyed boy picks me up in his arms by his cabin and runs down the hill to the water, laughing, threatening to throw me in. I laugh, too, and plead, though I don't know what I am pleading for. His skin is so close to my own. He has grown so much this year—freckled, chestnut, and always laughing. He is holding me audaciously in his arms. His chest, his arms, are my secret pleasures, like the best part of the inner earth erupted and clasped around me. Where is the rangy boy inside of me who would have already punched his way free; where is the haughty girl who will condescend to be admired but never touched? The clean smell of his shirt has lulled them. I want to rest here in respite of who I've come to be.

"I think I'll be coming up there for a week this summer. We should get together!"

We are finally kissing in the sparkling-eyed boy's black Toyota pickup truck. He has pulled down the dirt road to the dump so we can look for bears, but now he calms the headlights, soothes the engine, and finds my mouth by the light of the stars. The skin on our lips, the wetness inside of our mouths are actually touching. The field between us is permanently violated. His fingers are in my hair, wrapped around my skull as if the outer shell were merely for crushing: baby fingers, soft baby skull. Here is my baby hand; here is his baby cheek. We are just babies through and through.

Only we are not. We are seventeen and eighteen and for the first time, in this moment, we love each other equally and well.

With my skull having been clasped in such a way, is it any wonder that my brain would answer, "seventeen, *seventeen*" were someone to ask, How old do you feel now? And now?

"Affectionately,
Amy"

Guttering

The moon is the heart of the love of the world, I say from my dusty patch of grass next to my rented house in New Jersey — the Garden State, one long strip mall, one spreading cancer red zone. *It wells in compassion, dries into a slivered ache, and wells again.*

But the stars, oh, the stars are ever-dim, separated from me by more than light-years. Tonight I feel most acutely their feeble blurring. I have said occasional, hateful things to the sidewalk, the mirror, my date, because they won't quiet the lights of the refineries for even one night. The starflecks in my veins are guttering out, and I am stumbling into walls, buying fashion magazines.

Tonight I cannot say, *Isn't it sad and funny and incontestable that we are piercing our eyes with streetlights and headlights and city lights and letting them bleed all over our sunken cheeks.* Tonight I must put away irony because my heart is a sliver of an ache.

It is impossible to know the truth of the stars, to know the secrets of a leaf, to know how you look to anyone else in the world. It is impossible, that is, to keep your bearings once you have asked where you are. And yet, I can't help but think that the sparkling-eyed boy has the wisdom of an insider. In my memory, his movements are sure; his heart is round and full, far as he is from bright clusters of humans. He lives with the stars and the trees and the water inside himself such that he needn't ever think of them or even see them, as one might live and die in the same place without ever finding it on a map. Why fumble about for what is inside, holding your organs in place.

I was only a visitor to the stars, though, and the trees and the lake, the reeds, the mud, the sumac, the tamarack, the mint, whitecaps, cedar, wintergreen, bracken, micah, silt, seaweed, and the stars, the stars. Every summer night I walked home from my grandparent's cabin down the path, my head tilted back, feet left to fend for themselves. This was my dessert, an endless bowl of sugar crystals, deeper than I could ever sink my spoon. I brushed my teeth outside in the field even as I choked myself on the stars' grainy thickness. But this was, as it turned out, a timed exercise, like a pie-eating contest. Someone held out a stopwatch every June and said: You have from now until September to have your fill. Over many summers, I stopped feeling a singing in my blood and little hairs raising on my arms at the sight of the sky. The sense that something important, dangerous, fathomless, must always be happening under such a sky, turned into a feasting, a gorging of sky to mouth, a race to fix starlight and portent in my blood. The sky was a showy display of plenty, a trembling nest of sparkle like a bramble quivering with ripe raspberries ready to fall and rot in the dirt. The first hint of death for me was the dimming of the sky come September, when I was again under the jurisdiction of vigilant suburban night lights. I learned that plenty had nothing to do with permanence, so the ripe stars had to be fixed in the bucket, eaten until the juice ran out the sides of my mouth and the seeds clotted my teeth. I learned the refrain: Take a last look, take a last look. It's going to be a long time.

I can count the number of stars, now, in the uneven rectangle of sky framed by my roof, the roof next door, the roof behind me, and the roof across the street. And I do count them several times in the approximately seven minutes it takes to smoke a cigarette. It's not difficult—there are only eight stars, and they take no comforting shape, no animal, warrior, or kitchen utensil.

The sparkling-eyed boy hardly ever looked up like this—small, steady sips for the boy with the well right next to his house. I rode home in his pickup truck with him one night, along the shore of Lake Huron. A rolling lake, it isn't the deepest of the lakes, not the warmest or the most dangerous, the rockiest or the most useful, but it is, to me, the happiest. Its name is a people, like the sound of a bird, like a particular gray clarity, like pink, green, white, auburn rocks among the gray. He suddenly pulled over, mid-silence, pulled me from the truck, carried me down to the wet sand, and sank down, holding me tightly about the knees. He was silently crying against my jeans, and I froze. I couldn't ask him why or touch his hair; I could only look up and find his heart resting in the Big Dipper, not a drop spilled. His mouth, the swath of Orion's belt; his eyes, the North Star; his dimples, multiplied and flung to each horizon; his nerves strung out along the Milky Way, shifting, changing, fading and brightening.

Is this what I want from the sparkling-eyed boy, then? I want him to have triumphed where I failed. I want him to be an emblem of what won't ever be possible: to be *of* the stars and not just a visitor to them, a longer for them. It was important, dangerous, fathomless, to stand over a crying teenage boy turning himself inside out on the sand. But I merely watched as if I were preserving the moment instead of living it. Time—the things we think it takes from us—allows us the dramas of our lives: Take a last look, take a last look. It's going to be a long time.

Witness, Summer 1996

I spent my summers in the woods and the water and in the reeds somewhere in between. I staggered everywhere, drunk on sunlight and the colors green and blue, covered in burrs, mosquitoes, leeches, holding everything up to my nose with violent fingertips, tasting things that grew on the ends of branches. I carried heavy objects like logs, rocks, stringers of drooling fish, until my arms were round and freckled. I walked over grass and rocks and bees and rusted nails until my soles were too thick to know better. I knew the insides of milkweed, cattails, bull rushes, and gooseberries better than I will ever know anything.

Every Labor Day, when I had to return to school, I begged to be left up there instead of returning to Detroit with the rest of my family. It didn't work. In a vigil of mourning, I pressed my face to the car window during the seven-hour drive home, watching blankets of pine turn into fields, turn into house upon house, my chest heaving on emptiness. I hoped I would quit breathing entirely when we pulled into our driveway, but my lungs managed to crinkle and swell, crinkle and swell. I wanted to prove my loyalty by being permanently inconsolable, even by the porch swing, my favorite part of the house. That, too, never quite worked. I became well practiced at di-

viding myself into pieces, my favorite piece cut out every fall
and set aside until the next summer.

I went to college and left that self behind to carry on without
me, reeling under the pines. For four years I didn't even go back
to visit, my pale and tender feet safe in black socks and heavy
shoes. And this very fact terrifies me — that we could love so
wholly and so variably. We are dangerous, it seems, walking
around with so many, many selves catching and refracting the
light or lying pale and eyeless in the caves of us. How can we
hope to love any thing or person in the same way forever, or expect them to love us? How can we ever even explain ourselves
or account for our actions in transparent language?

There was a boy I left, too. You know him as the sparkling-
eyed boy; I knew him that way, too — he liked to kill warm animals with his bow and arrow. He liked to fish with hooks and
hand-held nets and lose himself in the woods on his four-
wheeler. He liked to lay his hands on things and transform
them: wood into furniture, ripe hay into bales, my hand into
his hand. He used to say he would never live in a trailer, he
wanted to go to school, he could see himself teaching shop.
But I couldn't imagine him somewhere else, losing any part of
himself, having to make himself up from scratch.

Seven years after I'd last seen them together — this boy, this
place — we met again, and I am desperate to remember any
clear detail about this first meeting. It seems that the moments
we'd most like to play, rewind, play, rewind, and play again
until the tape runs thin are the moments most unreliably
recorded. In these first few reunions with the sparkling-eyed
boy, I can see the participants, watch their lower jaws drop and
reconnect, tongues moving subtly against their teeth, but I can
hear nothing, and they look like they're under water and I'm
holding the wrong end of a telescope up to my eye.

· · ·

I can tell you what I remember.

Exposition: I was twenty-five and visiting the Upper Peninsula for a long summer weekend with my sister and her young
daughter. I had taken no time off from school—I was freshly
graduated from a three-year MFA program and about to enter
a Ph.D. program. I didn't know who I was besides a student,
but I thought I knew who the sparkling-eyed boy was. He had
stayed and been preserved in tar. He was a living fossil to me,
held up to a tawny light, named, well documented, carried in
my pocket as if I had the right to rub my fingerprints over him
or bury him in my palm.

The dreams featuring him had begun a few years before and
were the kind that filter into your day, your week, and make
you feel a mist of well-being and then the sudden, clammy loss
of it all at once. Eventually, he began to become a small part of
my writing. My friend joked that I had found a muse. And he
drove a pickup truck.

Rising Action: About a month before our visit, I wrote him
that awful letter ("I can't believe it's been seven years! Can you?
So much has happened!") all sterility and exclamation points,
as if I had been settling accounts before my death, smoothing
the way for a terminal visit. ("We've been friends for a long
time. Your wife won't mind if we visit, right? Let's get together!") And then, when I was actually there, I did nothing. I
was too scared to call him, to find out how he had reacted to
the letter, to how I'd left him without word, and to the seven
years I'd been away. I was going to let this visit slip past and let
myself slip into yet another collection of selves without finding out how this old one might have finished.

But my sister knew nothing of the regrets, the dreams, the
stories, and she's always had the knack for talking over awkwardness, so her tongue intervened. I found myself in the spar-

kling-eyed boy's best friend's house, sitting rigidly in a chair, a patchy smile on my face. His friend was on the phone: "Hey ——, whatcha doing? . . . I told you I'd help you do that backhoeing tomorrow night. . . . Yeah, after we finish with the O'Dair place. . . . So get your ass over here. Bring ——, too. We're havin' some beers. . . . Guess what. The Benson girls are here. [I cringed at how that turned us into caricatures, an after-thought — easily summed up, easily dismissed.] . . . Yeah, both of them, Janet and Amy. Okay, see you." A few minutes later I managed to ask, "So, are —— and his wife coming over?"

I think I went to the bathroom three times in the twenty minutes before they arrived. My hair, naturally a light brown, was dyed black then and was straggly from a day at the beach, my lipstick had gone the way of the lake, and my eyes were bloodshot — like a dog's at the vet. I didn't want to come out of the bathroom: I tried brushing my hair with his friend's wife's brush, ratting it into some kind of shape. I tried running cold water and pressing my chilled fingertips to my eyelids. Sure there was no feature he would recognize, I wished I had the sharp edges of a nametag on my T-shirt: "Hi! My Name Is Amy!" But I had to come out, and there he was — tall, almost grown-up-looking, married, with a six-pack of Budweiser and a terrible mustache. But that smile — he was smiling the smile I always thought was just for me. It was the only manifestation of the joke we'd been sharing since I was eleven and he was twelve. His deep dimples, his crinkled eyelids, told me we were still sharing it and it was still funny. Apparently, I *need* someone to look at me like that — even when it's meaningless, even when it's cheap or dangerous — because I was suddenly smit-ten in a way I hadn't known I was when I was seventeen. I didn't have a name for it then, and so I'd let that self sift through my fingers. Though at this first reunion I could have named the feeling I had when the sparkling-eyed boy walked through the door *nostalgia* or *anxiety about my uncertain future,* or, worse, *proprietorship,* I chose to call it *love.*

Denouement: My sister and I haven't always gotten along as we've learned to do over more time, and that weekend we had been waiting for the other to flinch or pout or smile funny, or sigh and say, "Nothing" when the other asks, "What did you say?" — or, in other words, to give each other any excuse to say, essentially, "Everything I've thought about you is true. You're still the same old harpy, the same priss, the same hothead, the same privileged mouse." We fell into it the next day. Technically, she ambushed me: she got me to ask, "What?" *Nothing.* "No, really, what?" *You think you're better than everyone; you're totally conceited, everyone can see that; just look at how you were last night, holding yourself apart from everyone, barely talking.* This is how she sees me — covered over in a thin film of ice, my skin blue-streaked, my hair and lashes brittle, my teeth cold against my tongue. Was the sparkling-eyed boy a more generous witness? What self did he sketch into the chair in which I shrank? I'm sure he saw the hair he had known as sandy blond dyed black, the bright toenail polish, the "different clothes." Did he invent a life to go along with the accessories — a life that bore but little resemblance to my own: I was a lost sheep, hard and hurting. I had probably done things with my body, my mouth, my voice, that had put me beyond his pale. Or did he overlay me with my seventeen-year-old self and see me the way he might remember me? It takes courage to imagine all of someone's possible selves and to let them rub together uneasily. Was he that brave? I know I wasn't.

Climax: I can tell you the few things I do remember about that night. I remember watching the sparkling-eyed boy's every gesture, trying to memorize each one for what I knew would be another long absence. I followed the tips of his eyelashes closing over his eyes and pressing back into his smooth eyelids. I watched his long fingers slipping on the sweat of his beer bottles. I trailed him at a distance as my sister took him into the bedroom where my niece was sleeping, watched him pull the blanket back from her face and say, "She's a cute little bean, isn't she?" I remember worrying that I was obvious to everyone there, that after I left his wife would banish me and his friends would laugh about my spilled love, messy, down the front of my shirt. I remember his wife talking to his friend's wife and only cursorily responding to my questions about her job teaching second grade (did she think I was mocking her?). I remember wearing a shortish skirt and having a shockingly thick clutch of bruises cascading down one thigh to below the knee from carrying buckets of rocks the day before and letting the pail bang against my leg. I was glad to have them. I thought he might find them charming proof that I was still staggering between water and land, an indestructible tomboy. I didn't foresee at the time that they might add to a general picture of urban disrepair—perhaps I even had an abusive boyfriend in the wings. He asked about them: "What happened there?" I wanted him to kneel in front of me and lightly trace the bruises, starting at my inner thigh and twisting down my outer calf and back again. He could have, maybe, pressed his mouth to them, tasted the lake water on my skin, and, like an animal, recognized me as one of his own.

This is, I realize, where I have gone wrong. I left that self in this place without a sturdy coat or the hope that she would ever see me again. What did I think would happen? Did I think this boy would come look for me and bring me home? I left him before I knew that in a real love, the bruising and healing, the leaving and returning, are constant—they happen hundreds of times a day. But the sparkling-eyed boy and I, all we know is the bruising, all we know is the leaving.

PART II

A Few Fictions About Desire

Somebody tells a story, let's say, and afterward
you ask, "Is it true?" and if the answer matters,
you've got your answer. —TIM O'BRIEN

Choking on It, Summer 1998

*O*nce, *smugly, I held my chubby cat above her just-filled food bowl and watched her four legs circle in the air like a desperate, mechanical baby's, tiny grunts leaking out of her face. I wish that if we must hunger, we don't hunger like that.*

I used to protect myself from the greedy hands of boys and the fever they might ignite in my own hands. I called it independence. I called it clever and focused. I didn't call it fear.

Now, on my way home from work I notice a new crevice down my arm. It is deep and chalky — the separation of dry skin from skin, dried blood from blood. I have never before in my life so needed to be touched and yet been so untouched. I will have to take care of my umbrella; the next rain might wash my powdery marrow away.

My sinuses are cracked and bleeding: a drop falls by the discount bookstore, a drop on the crushed sidewalk in front of the dry cleaner. My nose is caked and crusted by the time I reach my block.

It's been six months since my last relationship ended. He was sweet and smart and funny and he never touched me with a voracious hand. He almost never touched me. Sometimes I wanted to shake him or hit him. I still have a few items I bought in desperation then. One is my only negligee, a demure dark blue number worn once.

I am alone, and it seems the whole world has crumbled with drought: my bedroom walls leave smudges on my dark T-shirts; as I walk home, pieces of brick and tile, road sign and marigold, flake away in serious, spiteful chunks. My eyes have become gummy with longing, and I am looking for sympathy in the things around me.

This spring, two children in the neighborhood have attached themselves to me — Sam and Rosie. At the moment I live in one of the poorest neighborhoods in New Jersey, where I am conspicuously white. Sam and his sister are Haitian, and Sam tells me about his father, who lives in the next town with some woman and practices witchcraft. Sam is not yet in high school and has a crush on me. I'm flattered — I like it, even though I'm quite sure he's gay and flirts by coveting my shoes and nice-smelling shampoo. I take him to a local diner for his confirmation and let him order a sundae the size of his head, though the aunt he lives with wouldn't like it. He pounds on my door one night and tells me, laughing but with a hint of I-don't-want-to-know-what in his eyes, that someone he didn't know had just tried to get him into his car. I let him inside until I think the danger has passed. That one danger, at least.

I plant a garden for the first time as an adult, and it gets hotter and never rains — one of the driest summers in many years. Reservoirs are being burned up; the whole state is feverish. The kids come over for Popsicles and to help with the garden, but they do more harm than good and I try not to get annoyed. The fruits of the garden, when they come, are small and impenetrable. Sam comes over and I try to slice a tomato, but the drought has stunted it, thickened its skin and pulled it too tightly around it. I tell Sam it's still good on the inside, but neither of us can eat it. The metaphor may seem contrived, but this is how things really happen sometimes.

Soon, at the end of the summer, I will take a teaching job in a very small town in Missouri. Again, I will leave one life for another; I will leave Sam to men in cars, leave my collapsing garden, leave any opportunity for sex with or without love. This fever in me is growing septic. Where are the hands that could palm my stomach carefully, hold my head down to the mattress, a bulb watered with sweat? Where is the bewildered stroke of tongue or finger that circles and circles and never lands precisely on satiety? I had been so careful as a girl not to let desire rule me.

Desire is waiting for you in a book that would change your life if only you were ready for it. But you are never ready. It looks good on your shelf, and occasionally you dust the bookcase carefully.

I would touch myself, but that would probably only make me cry. So I return again to the scene I have imagined before: We are eighteen, nineteen, and experiencing sex for the first time in the upstairs room of the cabin the sparkling-eyed boy rebuilt with his own hands. I can't smell guilt in the air, not even the slightest whiff of sneaking. Rather, tenderness turns in the turning of our limbs. Our muscles and calluses are delicate ribbons and knots to one another. My hands slip on the sweat of his hips. I wish I could cut off the hollows around his hip bones and keep them with me forever. Between us are many freckles, many portals to the shyest, most elusive nerves; he is licking the brown flecks on my skin, leaking his DNA into each one of my pores. We stare; we press and gnaw with our eyes. We are not afraid to open our lids to what we haven't seen before, to accept a new memory for the rest of our lives. I am not afraid of my own folds reaching wetly into the center of my body.

Though my hands are clumsy with it, I am not afraid of the blooming head of his cock pressing into me or the things he might say tomorrow to anyone who asks.

But I *was* afraid, and this never happened. The boy who should have been my first lover wasn't nearly finished with the cabin he rebuilt with his own hands. That last summer I helped him pound tarpaper and shingles into sloping roofs. We touched each other in our sweat, and traced the path of its rivulets only as far as the snaps on our jeans. Then I went away and couldn't find any other sparkling-eyed boys who looked as if most of the world was delightful and I was most of all. So I held my T-shirt, my bra, my hands, my mouth, my neck, my hair, my eyes, and certainly the snaps on my jeans away from the world in which no one found delight. Rightly, wrongly, I saw danger everywhere. In men, yes, but in me, too, where desire could grow and grow and grow, making me ugly from the inside out. What have I done?

Desire is a lie told to yourself again and again about the texture of a boy and the amount of his skin you have felt against your skin, until the lie comes more easily than the truth, until the lie falls apart.

The City Mouse and the Country Mouse

You don't care what they say, it's hard to be the city mouse, always having to learn a lesson: Put away your extraneous baubles, city mouse, strip down to the bare necessities of mousehood—a pair of overalls, a straw hat and a stray weed in your mouth. The country mouse finds moral clarity in baling hay, shooting deer, and riding four-wheelers. Everyone sympathizes with the country mouse: Look at the city mouse, they say, struggling through the muddy path in her elaborate bonnet and her silver platforms. Shame on her horror at the outhouses, at the gas station-slash-video-slash-bait-and-tackle store. Isn't it unforgivable that when she visits, the city mouse makes the country mouse defensive and awkward for the first time? He mocks her university degrees even as he hides his grimy paws. What valiant dirt under each tiny claw. Don't let her push you around, country mouse.

But here's an odd thing: Is the city mouse lingering over the planes of his burnished face, over his paws, restless and dancing as he talks, his sure fingers, his clicks and grins, his sparkling, fresh-air eyes? What is that in her inscrutable city face? She fiddles with the ribbons at her throat; a tremor rolls through her whiskers. He is giving a treatise on fertilizer, another on bow hunting—there's more tension at the beginning of the pull and less when your thumb brushes your ear; just try holding steady on a distant speck; it's a difficult, difficult sport.

Look—the city mouse is nodding agreeably, making pleasant clucking sounds; she's curling her toe claws under to hide their blue polish; she's imagining sewing burlap dresses, standing over a fry pan brimming with venison. The country mouse is winning. He winks at her and her knees are weak. He spits his hay out the side of his mouth and beads of sweat appear around her muzzle. They have hours and hours until his country mouse wife comes home.

Look at her shimmy out of her Betsey Johnson sundress, out of her strappy sandals, out of her convictions about cultural imperialism, out of the corner of her bookshelf dedicated to lesbian feminist philosophy, her Modigliani prints—particularly the portentous nude whose nipple matches perfectly her orange vinyl chair, out of fists upon fists full of strange city mice she must brush up against every day, the perpetual clench of her jaw, her ability to change, her silver lipstick, her entire wardrobe, out of the nearness of others' stories, whole other mouse lives a wall away in every direction, that tattoo she never got, out of her love for all things in between, out of perpetual uncertainty until she stands perfectly naked, the touch of the world nowhere upon her, her tender under-fur quaking. She pretends that she has never had sex before and he is gratified.

Afterward, she reaches around on the floor for her sundress, her books, the clench of her jaw, her silver lipstick, but all she finds is a Penzoil T-shirt and a pair of jeans. She pulls these over her furred torso before he hustles her out of his house and to the end of his long gravel driveway.

He waves briefly and turns back to his field, the whole of the sky over his head. Haven't you learned your lesson, city mouse, in your Penzoil T-shirt, no place to go, no sparkly shoes on your feet?

A Fictional Journey in the Deep Midwest

Somebody's going to tell.

First there were miles and miles of corn, menacing field after field of wind's reflection. In wheat, hay, soybean, one is a fleshy beacon, one rises above. In corn, one is nothing.

But somebody's going to tell.

You drove north through Iowa moments ahead of a storm, the rain covering your scent, your heat, even the slight press of your tires on asphalt. You would have made a very clever fox. You chose the twistingest road through the tallest corn which rose and shivered and closed around your passing—a wall of dying green.

If you have an ally, let it be foliage.

Because somebody's going to tell. Somebody always tells when someone else makes a story. And then there is almost always triumph or scorn or outrage or cynicism or shame or condescension or anger or guilt.

. . .

Because with a whispered phone call the sparkling-eyed boy told you where he would be, you drove hours to the hunting camp where he, your now married childhood love, was holed up with men, his friends, fragrant and loud, bound by a constant, unswerving patter, as tender as lambs in their rough chins, as coiled as snakes in their silent, deadly rib cages. Here is their tobacco spit in cups; here is their pride at leaving their wives and driving across three states to kill birds. The sparkling-eyed boy sneaked out for one night because you were waiting in a ten-room motel, twenty miles down the highway.

You waited for hours in Room 8 without the comfort of individually wrapped cups or free soap. How many times did you brush your teeth and retouch your lipstick until the brownish red began to cake around the edges? How many times did you lift up your sweater and hold your breasts in front of the mirror? How many times did you pat your calves for the first breath of stubble, run your hands up your thighs to see how you would feel to him? And still you waited. You wrote little notes and placed them around the room: one under the right-side pillow, one wedged between the chrome mirror and the cinder-block wall, one in Gideon's Bible under Song of Solomon, one behind the toilet. They were witty, wry, sexy. They gave the whole thing away, so you gathered them up and burned them on the gravel outside the door.

And then there he was, and you with ashes on your hands.

But somebody's going to tell, because drunk men always pee in the middle of the night. The sparkling-eyed boy's best friend, his cousin, his uncle, the boy with the terrible stutter they take along for amusement, drifted awake one by one to the great pressure of their bladders and shuffled out to piss off the front porch. The first time out they may not have consciously noticed the troubling flatness, the absolute stillness of the wool blanket over the sparkling-eyed boy's bunk. On the second or third trip, surely a vague awareness stumbled in, a hazy question: *Where is he?* Certainly his best friend was puzzled. But it's not like these boys to worry, to wake each other in a flurry of urgent speculations, to need to know *anything* immediately. Just a simple question followed his friend down as he returned to sleep: *Where could he be?*

He sat down beside you on the curb and you looked at each other until you forgot to speak or blink. You kept looking at each other because you couldn't stop. But don't mistake this for love or longing. It was truly animal — that is, blank, uncomprehending. *What is this thing before my eyes?* your faces seemed to say. *A nose, the collar of a shirt? They mean nothing to me.* That ice machine, that clump of weeds, have more goodness and purpose than any two trapped in this particular deadlock. There is a reason why people blink, you realized, why they talk and nod and smile. You looked at this shape in front of you and you thought, *Why speak, why fuck, why drive, why eat, why work, why read, why have a list of things you need to decorate your house, why move, why breathe, why write?* Then he touched your cheek and said your name and you accidentally smeared ashes on his hands and gave him all the meaning and reason in the world.

Then there were eyelid kisses, yards of delighted skin, embarrassed laughter, breath in your hair, hair in your fingers, fingers covering your wrists, stories of the past, tongues running dry, and not one word about the future. You made a nest and lined it with ten years' worth of feathers in five hours.

But somebody's going to tell because people can be very grabby, yes, very greedy, indeed. And if you leave your nest for even a moment, as everyone must, someone is bound to discover it. And though it is still warm and fragrant, they will move in and immediately set to rearranging the feathers. They will see your nest as a mess you have made and will carefully label the exhibits of godlessness, of desperation, and really, if you think about it, of sheer pathos. They will grind the small bits of down and straw under their indignant heels. They might even douse the whole thing with gasoline and set it ablaze, regretting only that you are not trapped inside. They will most certainly talk and poke and bother until you are no longer able to pick your little story out of a lineup. Until you hate it.

You left the motel when he left, unable to stay in that room alone, unable to be the one left behind, no matter the richness of your life. You left your story, your damp nest, and agreed to be a part of someone else's story, because someone always tells.

You drove home, south, back into the belly of the country, down. And it was fall and that was just a coincidence, but my god everything was dying around you — the corn, the light, your smile, your pride, your conviction that no matter what, you would never do anything really, really bad. You would. You would kill to make this story your own, to keep just one brief eyelid kiss, to make believe any moment in this trip really happened. But on the outskirts of town, under the hard morning light, all truth in this story withered and fell.

Dearest Boy,

(Take 1)

I could love you like a fossil, a bit of stuff caught in a gesture held forever, valuable simply because it *is* and it has survived. My gesture would be a hand held to your cheek with all the adoration that hand might feel for that cheek, but it will last, held in mud, turned to stone.

I could love you like a spotted touch-me-not, my delicate or-chid heads bobbing in the wind, my arms rich with juices. And under my leaves, small sacks that, if touched, snap and curl and shower their seeds. If you came down this gravel road right now and touched me — it wouldn't matter where — I would turn inside out like that, in an instant.

I could love you like a hawk with a smooth brown head, signifi-cant claws, and a chest you might consider proud. Sometimes you will notice me, a stain against the sky. But mostly I will be very quiet, buoyed by air, until, my eyes having never wavered, I am upon you, tasting your heart.

I could love you like a poplar tree, trying hard to catch your eye with the silver undersides of my leaves. When the wind blows

them up, the whole of me is aflutter, flashing just for you. I am
hopelessly feminine. It does no good to blush, though. Men
will call my wood junk no matter what.

Or, most likely, I could love you like an island, something
welled up from the deep. I am all alone, surrounded by not-my-
kind, and missing you. But I can grow my own species — a
coarser marsh grass, a deeper blue to my spruce, and brand-
new beaks on birds I teach to sing nothing but your name.

PART III

Toward That Oxymoron, a Personal Ethics

Ornamental Nature

I guess when I was a kid I thought nature happened only when it could lie down, stretch out, and exhale acres of trees and clear, open water. Farms weren't nature; neither were city parks, and certainly not the suburban scalps of grass we all showered with chemicals and weekly shaved down to bristle. When nature got too close to humans, it seemed to fester with secrets about how we were all one breath away from falling down and letting the roots of a tree or that stifling network of grass climb over us. And so, momentarily having the upper hand, we cut it, hemmed it, powdered it, and pinned it up.

I hated the shrubs around my parents' suburban Detroit house: sharp, pungent juniper, square yew with their red berries sticky when crushed — their skins, much more vulnerable than ours, gave at the slightest touch. They oozed onto the sidewalk in a mess of a bad omen that couldn't be swept up and drew clouds of ants. The point at which the walls of suburban houses meet the lawns is apparently unseemly and must be covered up with these stunted trees. They are forever circling, circling. When we look at a shrub we should see a wolf in a zoo, a Lothario in a marriage — things made sad and mean in confinement.

I wouldn't have noticed, I suppose, if the Upper Peninsula

hadn't taught me to compare so ruthlessly. The stunted cedar tree at the corner of our suburban Detroit house smelled like death to me; it hunkered darkly, full of spiders. Up north, the same cedars, multiplied and swollen, together formed the darkest part of our forest; their bodies had a velvety look, their hairy bark barely hanging on, their scent all shadow and spike. I was a visitor to their drama, these progenitors of fairy tales — and the story changed with the trees, the background music from minor to major. The cedar and balsam rose to spruce and white pine, which rose further to a happy ending of ridge peaks with birch and black-eyed Susans and sunlight, pale as butter, reflected off the powdery trunks. Except for the trail, which we cleared of fallen trees and brush, we left things as they were because the forest was not our story. I admired the patternless angles of fallen or half-fallen trees, the race to fill gaps where sunlight shot through the canopy, the random surging of limestone through the soil.

Children are desperate for mystery, for a world to stumble into that is bigger than the one they've known, that tells them they might never get to the bottom of it. The suburbs are not, in fact, a safe place to raise children. They are a carefully arranged netherland that prunes out chaos. We tend our parcels of land and shelter, and our imaginations stop at our lot lines, the end of our ownership. I didn't know as a child that it was fashionable to decry suburbs, but I felt keenly the hubris of choosing shrubs and flowers, then planting and pruning them to precisely the size and shape we wanted. Up north, the inconsequential role we humans seemed to play in the larger drama was no secret — humans perched on the edges of forest, shore, ice, island. They ate fish, venison, blew limestone and dolomite up out of the ground, tore through the woods on snowmobiles and four-wheelers. They built small houses or parked trailers in the fields near woods and planted vegetable gardens they could barely keep from raccoon, deer, and frost. They tucked away tourist oddities, like The World's Largest Seashell Collection and The Mystery Spot, into the forests; they sometimes put lawn ornaments featuring the rumps of large old ladies in front of their houses; they left old refrigerators, boats, and propane tanks behind their barns, and burned everything else at the county dump — kitchen trash, tires, batteries. Often, they didn't pave roads or name them. But they didn't seem to plant shrubs or build ornamental mounds or asphalt nature trails. They just lived with nature, in it, sometimes carelessly.

I loved everything about that place. I thought that to step lightly was good, to erase yourself completely and start over in a dream of a garden in which no human decision had yet been made, no fingernail yet torn a leaf, was best. And I was unborn there, prehuman, a pair of eyes, an unhinged mind. I knew it. And it was good.

But it is then difficult to grow into a world full of so many people and their miniature beauties, and the small patterns they impose on the malleable things around them. My inheritance from summers up north was a conviction that it is better to let the things that spring out of the ground create you than to create them, it is better not to know the end of the story than to have written it yourself, it is better to hate your home and its square shrubs than to let your mind waver and then shrink.

And yet I know that we are always writing the story, especially when we try so hard not to, especially when we think we love nature. I know that the current recommended yearly allowance of Great Lakes whitefish is one serving, and that we ate the fish we caught almost every night. We could not imagine mercury, PCBs, DDT, penetrating our wild place and drifting into the bellies of fish. I know that my lakes, Huron and Superior, are clear and cold and perfect and as polluted as any fetid, shallow pond. I know that as close as we were to Canada, I must have been standing out in torrential downpours of acid rain. I know that my favorite part of the forest, the birch ridge, is not our land and could be, if the owner wanted, fenced off or cut down at any moment. I know that I edit out the other cabins down the road and the ocean liners and ore boats that loom past in the channel of the St. Mary's River because they don't fit the mental picture I like best. I know now a new corporation might dig a limestone quarry just a mile down the shore from us and across from Lime Island, which hasn't wholly healed from its earlier gutting in the mid-1900s. I know that the entire Upper Peninsula was logged to nubbed dirt little more than a century ago, that "virgin timber" is a quaint phrase. I know that our national parks have borders, and bears addicted to junk food, and entry fees, and the sharp elbows of tourists like me. In other words, I know how much fantasy there is in the word *nature* and I know how much we have constructed this world, shrubs being the most benign example. And I know if there were such a thing as a wild place, we would remake that, too.

Much is made of the imaginations of children — how fertile, how powerful, how inspiring. Perhaps we're wrong about them; perhaps their imaginations are not more potent than ours. When we grow up, the world shrinks to the size of our own brains, and we must imagine ourselves delighted. We have to work so much harder to imagine the products of our hands bearable, to gather enough small strips of beauty to tie into a rope that holds. The Japanese maple at the end of my block is not cold and far away from home; the potted plant on the back of a bicycle moving down Eighty-second Street is lovely.

Funeral

First it was the monarchs. I was six and thought that the world was finally right when the butterflies descended. They were melodramatic in their numbers, obscene. The air was thick with them, fanning my sun-fevered skin with their wings. Everything was at once uniformly ablaze, pulsing in the same orange and black. When I lifted an arm or kicked a leg, I could raise up a hundred flutters. But then they began to die. Our little gravel road — the one with the grassy center and two wheel ruts — became one great clot of twisted insects. The bodies of dead butterflies deflate and shrivel, their wings disintegrate from the edges in. I remember picking up a few and tossing them into the air, willing them to twitch their wings, pretending I really didn't understand death.

Some of us are born with a great capacity for nostalgia and idealism (which are actually two breeds of the same species). I was born willing myself to unknow almost anything I learned. And what the monarchs taught me was that, truly, the right amount of melancholy for the indelible sadnesses of the world is not available to us. I shed tears, stroked some of their wings, but then I took to the cabin rather than acknowledge a slackening of my grief.

· · ·

Six years later it was the frogs. Every summer a frog or two would get caught under a wheel on that gravel road leading out of our family land. Even though only a few cars go in and out every day, it was inevitable: the little road twists along the marshy shore that's home to many deep-throated water creatures. But that summer, the summer I turned thirteen, something was different. There were never fewer than six or seven dead frogs on the road at a time. I counted them as my sister and I walked to the county dock to swim with the boys. At least two new frogs were splayed on the road every day. They were perfectly symmetrical and stiff. If my sister and I had been boys, we might have picked up the bodies with the tips of our fingers and thrown them at each other — tiny, frog-shaped Frisbees. If they had caught a good thermal, I imagine these flattened frogs might have glided off into the bull rushes, down into the water, which would reconstitute them too late. But since we were girls, we stepped around them with our stone-callused feet.

None of the other local swimming boys ever came home with us from our daily trips to the dock. Encountering girls' parents — particularly our suspicious, old-fashioned parents — is simply more work than most young boys care to take on without substantial rewards. And so they roared away on their three-wheelers or piled into one of the boy's ancient pickup trucks, which no one was old enough to drive legally, and rolled back into the lives we would never quite share. The sparkling-eyed boy, however, became part of our lives. He walked back with us often, pushing his bike, my sister usually a few yards ahead of us, clarifying the pecking order. First sun and then water, wind, and then an exasperated, quick-tongued older sister, a tongue-tied, mooney younger sister, and finally a teasing, freckled boy with a crush who would, when he reached the girl's summer cabin, move rocks, stack wood, shovel dirt, weed the garden, or help with whatever other chores her father had lined up for them while they were away. Pleasure must be earned, and he worked, laughing all the while, to be the one "good kid," the faithful companion, the golden son-in-law, to be the boy next to the girl for the longest.

I suspect if he'd been alone on the road and encountered that clutter of dried-up frogs, he might have kicked them absentmindedly, or even put some real effort into it, found a stick and hit them like hockey pucks. But he wasn't alone. He was with me. And I decided one day that such a holocaust could not pass unnoticed. For life to remain precious, I must have reasoned, the least scrap of it — down to these hardened slices of amphibian, their deep glugs flattened in their throats — must be mourned. I probably thought that I was a very soulful young lady; I probably hoped that everyone else would think so, too.

But in truth, I was motivated more by fear than by image. I was afraid that I actually felt nothing, that I could have gleefully kicked every single frog from one end of the road to the other just for a moment's amusement. I was willing myself not to know what was all around me: little deaths everywhere (just look at the living branches I casually snapped on walks through the woods; the broken cedar waxwing eggs; the walleye's mouth hooked clean through, my proud eyes). I was avoiding the knowledge that to notice any particular death more than any other is to indulge in pointless, self-serving pathos. In another time, say seventy years ago, this rage of mine to unknow what I knew would have made me an excellent German haus frau, serving up painstakingly etched eggcups and daily airing out my feather ticks, inhaling all the while the scent of scorched flesh.

Instead, with perfect repression, I told the sparkling-eyed boy that we should hold a funeral for all of these frogs. The key, I knew, was ritual. In order to be sure, sure you understand, that the stray threads of emotion and thought that made up our brains mattered, that we were not going to dissolve and become something else in moment (a flap of skin, say), that we were even alive, we needed to make our response to these frogs public, if only to each other. We needed to be appreciated. We needed a ritual. The sparkling-eyed boy could have teased me, as he often did, but he too made a decision in that moment. We would have a funeral. We probably gathered tiny flowers out of the ditches, moved with bloated stateliness, and said a few words over the frogs, having learned early that every ritual must have a script. And then we launched a little barge of the dried carcasses into the river. We sat and watched the barge drift off in the wide, almost currentless St. Mary's River until we could no longer make out the dark spot on the water. It was thrilling and pathetic at once: two small human beings at the end of a dock, compelled by gravity, shocked to have made meaning on their own for once, shocked at how hollow it was.

We were both pretending to save our souls, pretending that we weren't too old for this silly display, that we hadn't already learned a different truth about death — that it's far too easy to care not at all — and a different truth about the meaning of our lives — that we couldn't give each other what we really wanted, no one could, not for long, anyway. And he was pretending that because he had gone along with me that I loved him best, and I was pretending that I didn't. So there we were — a pathetic liar and her accomplice. I think I could either thank him or apologize to him for the part he played.

I don't know which species died en masse six summers later, or six more summers after that, because I wasn't there. What I do know is that I haven't changed a bit. I am still willing myself to unknow what I know: people grow up; one identity disintegrates as another is forged; people don't love each other forever; just because I write it doesn't make it so. I am creating the most elaborate shrine to unknowing I can imagine. No, I haven't changed a bit: here I am, a liar and her accomplice.

My Sister

The sparkling-eyed boy did not love my sister. He loved knowing things. He loved basketball, lathes, making up names for people (Dudley, Fishack, Chicken), cheating with me at euchre, the drama of his own constancy. But he didn't love my sister.

She curved in circles of eyeliner and shiny red belts. She wore plastic sunglasses in the shape of hands and painted her lips in fierce colors. She had never been mistaken for a boy. She said things like "T and A" and wouldn't tell me what they meant. Her first instinct was to lie, but she was more than willing to confess. She took a lot of blame that both was and was not really hers. She taught me how to sneak home after our curfew on summer nights, inching the car's tires along the popping rocks, the headlights turned off. We barely breathed. Was she thinking about bruising pressure on her lips? About the syrupy tang of peach schnapps and orange juice that matched, somehow, her heavy red-brown hair? Did she wish I weren't there? I wouldn't have been late if it hadn't been for her. She spoke like a girl who likes most boys, who understands them, who thinks they're funny, who knows just what they're up to. She spoke for me because I couldn't possibly have spoken for myself. She let me hold the wheel of the car sometimes as we sped over the ice-broken roads up north. When she stroked a mascara wand over her curled lashes, her face caught in the rearview mirror, I felt as if I was watching a music video. She lived her life and I watched. She gunned for a seagull with her car once, screaming with laughter, but she didn't expect to hit it. We saw a cartwheel of feathers fly up from the back bumper. She hit a deer once, too. And she didn't cry—not because she was cruel (she wasn't), but because she was honest. The only thing she pretended about was how little she needed anyone to love her. And at night? After midnight she hissed and flamed over the night sky and fell to the earth in a field of sparks I'd swear would set something on fire.

Even though she knew she was officially the "bad sister," she had a hard time knowing where she stopped and I began. So sometimes she hated us both. She wanted me to know—really know—that my body was too ugly for any boy to really love me, that I acted like I was forty and eight at the same time, that most nights she didn't want me anywhere near her. She wanted to scald me with words that made her own mouth blister. I didn't know where she stopped and I began either, so I mourned her lost innocence as I would have mourned my own. I imagined those boys' hands on *me,* their spit in *my* mouth. Only, I added too much smirk, beer, fumbling, averted eyes. And I didn't know to add joy and the delicious liquifying of tongue to tongue, part to part. And I didn't know to shimmer like something exploded, flung and showering, unmindful of place and name, a million glimmers at once, big.

I'd sit waiting in a car, on a picnic table, around a fire. Often the sparkling-eyed boy would be sitting next to me, both of us with our hands in our pockets, very, very small inside. It was as if we could see the whole of our lives at once, all around us, and wanted to get it exactly right. Only, we were so careful our lives evaporated.

Once, in the second summer we went out, he asked me if I was really a virgin. He said so-and-so said I couldn't be with a sister like mine. I should have told him that my sister was a blue flame — the beautiful, pure heart of fire. I should have told him it was none of his fucking business. But I said, "That's exactly why I am. I don't want to be like her."

The sparkling-eyed boy may have loved me, but he didn't love my sister. And I, I didn't love her enough.

Sociology, That Soft Science in Us All

There is something deep in our American culture that says what is new is what is best—the fresh maverick, the urbane newcomer. Like teenage anarchists, we were founded on the leveling of old and ancient cultures—Native American, English, African, French—and the installation of replacements—genocide, democracy, slavery, industrial invention. We were, are, blinded with newness. In my generation, if you haven't moved away from home, or if you return home to live, you are a loser. At best, you feel you must apologize for your stuckness. We who leave arrive at our next place and size up its social disharmonies, never feeling as if they are our own.

Divisions of race and class often flower malignantly out of attachment to place—the other group occupies a place or province (mental, physical, cultural) we would like to have for our own, and so we hate them. Or they remind us of our past usurpings and so we hate them. And for a visitor, these divisions are terribly easy to diagnose. I could see that the locals I grew up with in the Upper Peninsula had to import their hostilities because the real conflict—the one with the locals, Ojibwe and Ottawa, who had been there before them—they

couldn't look directly in the eye. It was too close. Instead, they
talked about blacks and how they could never live in Detroit.
However, these locals, relative newcomers, were left with
boatfuls of quiet resentment over the Native Americans' gov-
ernment-funded reservations and special fishing rights. They
seemed to have an unspoken set of beliefs: Indians could fish
out of season, use nets that caught fish at the gill, just behind their panicked eye. Indians didn't care if the fish was big
enough; they'd keep it out of spite, its belly tight with unused
eggs. And they would eat anything: bones, scales, bowels. If
only the Indians realized, the locals seemed to imply, how much
they didn't deserve, how unnecessary their bird talk, clicking
tongues, and smoky breath, their deadly memories. I gleaned
this from a look here, an eye roll there, a sticky, targetless curse.

Though many of the locals lived below or near the poverty
line, they weren't violent in their sense of injustice. What I noticed, even as a girl there, was a quiet gulf. A second cousin of
mine who lived up there, a redhead with skin the same color as
the whites of his eyes, married a tribeswoman. Nobody treated
her badly, not even behind their backs. But they stopped talking
when she walked among us, almost as if she were already a
spirit or a sleek wolf, and they looked at her with wonder, unable to work the hinges on their jaws.

What I heard locals mouth off about in my summer visits were
the problems with which they had no experience — "white
flight" and the crumbling urban centers of places like Detroit
and Cleveland, Baltimore, St. Louis. When I returned for the
first time after college and saw some of the old crowd, I mentioned that I would be going to graduate school in the South.
Someone said, "Why would you want to go down there? Aren't
there a lot of blacks there?" And, though I had worn an alarm-
ingly sanctimonious button, "Poverty Is Violence," on my coat

for much of college, "So what?" was probably all I said in return. Instead, I later thought about those words sadly, angrily, smugly. And then I thought of something else.

Last summer some friends of mine from New York City came to the Upper Peninsula with me for a week's vacation. One night we went to the reservation casino outside of Sault Ste. Marie in a ha-ha, ironic gesture. And to play fifty-cent roulette, of course. In the green, forested U.P., this reservation seemed oddly parched and tree impoverished. To the locals, unfamiliar with the depressing uniformity of suburban track housing, I imagined, the reservation houses would seem uniquely claustrophobic. They looked fragile, as if the mold with which they'd been formed had grown thin with overuse. I don't know how the houses looked to the people who lived in them every day.

Once inside the casino/hotel/concert arena, the social chasms opened themselves easily to the eye:

The tourists come from the hotel, the tour buses, or the monstrous RVs in the parking lots. Their clothes are generally beige and too neatly pressed, and they check and recheck their hair with their fingers. They have a game, I'm-experiencing-something-new look about them as they consider purchasing a miniature tomahawk trailing turquoise and yellow chicken feathers. They split off to the slots or the highest stakes tables.

The locals — at least those who would consider themselves true locals, having not made too much money or chosen a too-fancy drink — sit under stiff polyester baseball caps, usually at the blackjack tables. They toss their chips on the felt, throw down their hands when the cards betray them, and lob comments toward each other, terse, witty little word chips. They don't meet the dealer's eyes.

And my friends and I are there in our comic shirts to emphasize the wackiness of being in a casino, on a reservation, in the

Upper Peninsula of Michigan. We have thought of every angle and we can't be fooled.

None of us here can help looking out of the sides of her eyes at anyone with burnished skin and cheekbones that could gut fish. They are the dealers and bartenders in shiny purple uniforms, and the tribal council in the enormous portraits hanging on the wall. I wonder what they think of the necessary tackiness of a casino, the way it bloats and dwarfs everything around it. Of all of the foolish white people and our tense version of fun.

Driving through blighted neighborhoods in Detroit as a teenager, I imagined how the city could be transformed if everyone who graduated high school from the metro area had to devote one year to fixing up the city before moving on to college or jobs. We could rebuild the burned-out mansions along Woodward, plant gardens, construct playgrounds, and raise money. The idea seems obviously naive now. Who would stay that long, who would know well enough what needed to be done? And who would be forced to have a stake in the city that raised them? It is far easier to move on than to be insinuated in the problems of your place.

I've never talked with anyone up north about these painful apertures between people. It's been my assumption since becoming transitory that you cannot *see* enough unless you are outside; and you cannot *care* enough unless you are inside. A lose-lose scenario.

But perhaps this isn't the case. How far back do you step before you lose the frame entirely? Perhaps being new means you see nothing accurately. How could we, with our campy, casino grins? The other day, walking through my own city neighborhood, I thought, This could be filmed as a portrait of "Urban Despair," and no one watching would know that we are mildly happy.

You, Only Worse, Summer 1993

Wedding videos are not meant for ex-girlfriends, girls who were inexorably part of you and then left and never came back. And they are not meant for strangers. Wedding videos document an impossible moment in which you publicly make a decision to be a particular someone for the rest of your life. The video should be made so that privately you can watch the moment over and over until it is real to you, but it should never get into the wrong hands.

The video is grainy, of course, the attendees awkward. But who is ever at his best at a wedding? Even the clergy often seem startled, scripted though they are. In the broad shots I recognize his father, who looks like a Scottish fisherman but is a high school teacher. I see a few of his friends from high school either lathering under a tie or trying not to touch their anomalously slicked-back hair. And I recognize the hole where his mother should be but isn't. She was the first one to leave him, and she stayed gone.

But I am twenty-one and having the fact of the sparkling-eyed boy's marriage made rather absurdly clear to me for the first time. I had carried with me a ludicrous faith, unconfessed even to myself, that he would have waited for me to come back around. Of course, I had heard of the match a year before, but part of me couldn't believe the sparkling-eyed boy would marry someone else, and only three years after I left. But there is his bride in brown sausage curls and a dress of sculpted meringue. The groom is nowhere in sight.

I did not set out to see the video, had not even known there was such a reel ten minutes before. My best friend at the time and I had shown up unannounced at the sparkling-eyed boy's best friend's house one evening four years after I'd last seen them. I suppose he didn't know what else to do with us, and so he made the most awkward, or perhaps the most spiteful choice—"Do you want to see a tape of ——'s wedding?" My friend, with a sharp eye for drama and the parts of the psyche that hurt the most when pressed, answered for me instantly.

We'd been close friends for years. But recently, we'd slowly broken each other's hearts into tiny shards ill-equipped for kindness. This would be her first and only trip up north with me, and we were pretending as if we were still trying to love each other like friends should. So, on our last night here, looking for some way to lay her hands on this part of my life I hadn't shared with her, she insisted that we look up some of my old friends.

We got only as far as the sparkling-eyed boy's best friend, still living with his parents. I believe none of us knew how to handle our losses with anything like grace. My friend was making me watch the video. And here I am, exacting my price. Do we have *any* moments on which we can look back with pride? I can't help but think that just by being, just by wanting and crying and smiling at the right moment and getting others to love us and need us and prop us up and carry us on and keep us from even five minutes of loneliness, we have already sullied our moments before we even live them. I'm talking not about god and original sin, but about nature—it holds too few examples in which the triumph of one is not a crime against another.

We can't help but try to cast the world in our own image, but there is always a cost for willfulness, desire.

The sparkling-eyed boy suddenly appears on the screen, reliving the moments of commitment again. He shifts his feet from side to side and looks as if he is trembling. My worst impulses hope the trembling comes from terror or reluctance or some premonition that I might someday watch him mouth these vows, the vows I imagined he once might have wanted to take with me. The sparkling-eyed boy's friend is stretched out on the shag carpet of his parents' den, not looking at me, though I know my friend is studying my face closely, looking for weakness in the shadows across my mouth. It was as if we'd had a contest throughout college to see who could be the least vulnerable. I was hopelessly in the red.

On the screen, the sparkling-eyed boy has turned his face toward me and I see his eyes and dimples and then—a *mustache* spreading across tanned skin, and I know it can't be the face of *my* sparkling-eyed boy. The mustache looks to me like a cheap disguise, taped to his shaking upper lip so he could shift his way to the front of the church and accept a life I don't want him to need. I see in the mustache on this boy's face how achingly he wanted to believe himself a man. But I could not imagine myself next to *this* man, sincerely kissing his nearly obscured upper lip, his ring heavy on my hand. Something had happened to him, but I felt I knew his better, clean-shaven self, and I could have saved him had I not been watching the ceremony on tape more than a year later.

Later, the night would get worse, seedy even. I would become more silent than usual and would watch my friend take over, aggressive with her brain, her body. We all drink too much at the one local bar, and my friend seems to make fun of the sparkling-eyed boy's best friend without him knowing it, and then flirts with him so that he can't miss it. We select the countriest country songs on the jukebox and play pool, circling each other like novice wrestlers in a ring. Still later, she presses us to go swimming, though it is after midnight and we have no swimsuits and all I can think of is the sparkling-eyed boy asleep with his wife in their marriage bed a few miles away, the hairs of his mustache pressed into her shoulder. My friend swigs from a bottle of Baileys, climbs down into the water in her underwear, and flings her wet bra up onto the county dock. I keep my sturdy underwear on, soaking them in lake water as I tread in the shadow of the big dock. I hiss at her to keep her voice down — sound travels so clearly over water — and she calls me a pussy for not having dropped my bra to the gravel. She floats her breasts on the water and turns them, round and impossibly white in the moonlight, their nipples pinched tight and purplish with cold, toward the boy. He laughs hard and mutters drunkenly to himself, saving up each detail for an apocryphal story to tell the sparkling-eyed boy the next day at their construction site — the one about what had happened to the girl he had once loved. And the sparkling-eyed boy, I imagine, would hear the story and think he had never really known the girl at all.

The world is treacherous, and we think we save some part of ourselves safe from other people. We are always better than they might imagine, the list of our hidden virtues and depths thick and cross-referenced. We always have some secret that would hurt them if only they knew. But who else knows this self? Who can corroborate our stories?

I thought the sparkling-eyed boy would *always* love my best self best, but here he is, in disguise, making a promise to love someone else for the rest of his life, his surface caught at it on

film. I want to be good, I really do. I want to believe in the ab-
surdity of my expectations, but I can't help but think the good
part of me disappeared when he stopped loving it best. And I
can't help wanting it back. So, the truth for now is this: We have
no best self; we are what other people see, all of them, only
worse. And the things we promise ourselves and the curses we
whisper at one another are not enough to keep us for our
whole lives.

The Moment After the Moment It
Would Have Mattered

I was, as always, conscious of my body. Bronzed Europeans sat around me on a beach on Crete, many of the women in bikinis, the top folded or flung to the towel beneath them. The women in one-piece suits had popped the straps off their shoulders and rolled the suits down past their bellies. Some of the breasts hung to the side, slightly deflated. I could see Greek men on the periphery, falsely deferential, cool and leering. These men and I had something in common. We watched — the men shrugging and smiling, me with my straps firmly in place. They felt the air on their breasts, these women. And those who swam? The salty Mediterranean dripped from their nipples and down into their bikini bottoms. It dried in sparkly streaks across their breasts. I saw it all, behind my sunglasses.

Didn't they know themselves interesting, watchable — maybe vulnerable in their skins? I would be hard-pressed to find one picture of myself in which I did not look as if a teacup would crumble to chalk in my hands. I am that cautious, tense, and poised. And I am not alone. Don't many Americans feel under surveillance, on audition, stalked? The faces of these women are different. They have built an independent meaning for themselves; they are not always about to be discovered.

But the sun set low, as suns do, and the women covered their bereft nipples, gathered books, blankets, baskets, and families, and left through hills of azaleas. Even the Greek men packed up their drink stands, and towels, and trinkets, their need, scorn, and boredom, and went home. I was alone with my blue-veined breasts and the poised tension of my hands. No audience.

In every landscape there is a focal point, and after the women left the point was a rock rising up like a fiery forehead, cooled, just breaking the surface of the still Mediterranean. People had been jumping from this rock all afternoon. They looked as if they were having fun. Now that they were gone, I paddled out to this rock. To my left the sun was bleeding into the water, but I could still see in the water on the other side of the rock where people had been jumping and diving all day, rocks under the surface, dark places where briny creatures could curl. I was simultaneously afraid of diving into this unknown under the darkening sky and of not diving and the subsequent withering of my life. This was a test, a precipice. If I could not bare my breasts or dive from this rock, I could no longer be an authentic person, a person who acts without thinking of a present or future audience. So I swayed on the rough pumice rock for a long time, watching my life shutter closed in the water below. Finally, I reached up and pushed a strap off one shoulder, then another, and then my cotton suit fell below my navel. I glanced quickly over my shoulder, but the beach was empty and the sea in front of me was one unbroken skin to mainland Greece. I dove in. I felt the velvet water palm my breasts and stomach, and the rest of my suit flutter against my thighs. I told myself I was saved, brand new. But as I paddled back to shore, pulling my straps up, the empty beach bespoke the emptiness of gestures. I knew I was long past the moment when any of this would have counted for bravery, for soul, even for nonchalance.

Life is full of such precipices. Just now, for example, I am standing at the edge of honesty, afraid to keep talking for what I might say. I have a story to tell, and, though I write and write about the sparkling-eyed boy, I haven't told it yet. To imagine doing so makes me feel naked, naked like a foot, like the red, wrinkled sole of a foot. And if I keep talking, I'll tell you things I never intended, which may, for just that very reason, seem like the only truth.

Once, as an undergraduate, I had to read at a feminist literary conference. My poem was long and it just happened to be about rape and there just happened to be a big crowd, so I was nervous and my voice shook as if I were on the verge of tears all the way through it. As if it were some kind of therapy session. I wanted to say, honestly, This is not me, it's made up! But for once I looked authentic. They had decided I was raw, laid open, uncensored. Self-consciously silent, I found my seat in a wash of eager or embarrassed sympathy.

He wasn't the sort of boy girls take to immediately. He was gawky and chatty and teasing. He wanted attention. He felt things, and—it seems an odd way to put this, since he's one of the only men I know now who does physical work for a living —he was almost feminine in this way. You could tell the cool, distant boys didn't respect him. They cuffed him on the head.

One moment my sister and I had been alone, together, thirteen and eleven, spending another summer in this wild corner of the Great Lakes, as we had done all of our lives, an occasional older cousin our only company. My grandfather, great-grandparents, and great-great-grandparents homesteaded there—a narrow survival few attempted. And the score was similar for us: a wilderness without people; one little girl, a second little girl, and many green and breathing creatures. Then suddenly we had a gang, mostly boys, mostly related to one another (and to us, we squirmingly realized years later — seventh or eighth cousins), mostly flirting with my sister. Our parents were horrified, their elder daughter clearly ripening. But, inexplicably to me of the sexy sister (how could the same swimming suit look so different on me?), the sparkling-eyed boy, distant cousin, geek, was always by my side. At first, I tolerated his liking me. I was one of those terrible girls who craves adoration but has no intention of being "caught" by her admirer. Worst of all, girls like me, they never admit that's what they're doing. We were "just friends," I would insist. We went on like this for years — I was trying to float, innocent, above the world, and if he couldn't understand the purer attractions of platonic love (read: of his unreturned devotion), then that was his problem. How early we're capable of tiny evils. How early we're able to need from little unstitchable wounds. But that's not the end of the story, not my final act of regret.

Five years later, the summer before my senior year of high school, things changed between the sparkling-eyed boy and me. My parents and I returned to that fishing camp in Ontario before going to our cabin. We drove forever on gravel roads, flew in a seaplane over thick rugs of evergreens that maybe no one will ever cut down. The year before, the sparkling-eyed boy and his best friend had gone with us, but they didn't have the money this year. Our guide, the same guide we'd had the year before, asked me where they were, asked, Isn't —— your boyfriend? "No." I laughed discreetly. "We're just friends." But I seemed to recall something of last year — his shadow cast over the side of our little aluminum boats. And the smell of pine needles and the cleanest water I have ever seen — I believe I confused those scents with him. Strips of electric light had bounced across our T-shirts, the water generous and indiscriminate with its beauty. We had been dressed up in nature: fish guts, wood smoke, pollen, lake-soaked jeans. He had carried me down to the water and threatened to throw me in. I could smell the heat of his chest, his neck, feel his arms pinching into my thigh, my rib cage, but gently, as if what he really wanted was to comb out my hair and feed me soup. "No. We're just friends."

But I cast endlessly that day, my legs hooked over the side of the boat, the rims of my ears bubbling under the sun, and wondered: What kind of friends are we? I caught a few bright fish, and I came up with an answer. I never laughed as much, or, lately, hardly at all, as I did with him. I missed him. I wanted him to tease me, to stick so closely to me that people mistook him for my boyfriend—until *I* mistook him for my boyfriend.

I think that there can be no *return* for constancy. *Payment* is not a word we should be allowed to use with one another. Let me tell you, back then I wore hair spray, my skin was awash in tiny taupe freckles, I was just discovering the Beatles years too late, my armpits usually smelled like baby powder. Back then he was already on his own, working for a drywaller in a nearby town, his grin was easy, there was fear zippered around the edges of his hazel eyes, he took two or three showers a day. What could we possibly pay each other? To avoid crushing each other's smooth-skinned selves, we would have to have been impossibly good. It is not possible to be that good.

So we came back to our summer home. We didn't have a phone line then, so any contact we made had to be visual. Thus, I looked for the sparkling-eyed boy. Or rather, I wanted him to know I'd returned so that he might look for me. I pictured some scene in which the sparkling-eyed boy, like an acolyte who's convinced of his lot in life, would take up his post by my side with the acquiescence of the perpetually rejected. I imagined being like a priestess, turning on him my eyes-too-bright-to-be-looked-upon, surprising, delighting him, making him eternally grateful with the return of his affections. How, I ask you, can you love when you see yourself as a prize to be awarded? Nevertheless, that's how it started: I suddenly realized that I *liked* the sparkling-eyed boy.

Of course everyone knows that experience is never as tidy as the stories we cull from it; and memory is even worse — it's just the story we tell ourselves enough times it sticks. But when we tell stories of love, we need plot points and explanations. If I were true to experience, I would stand here incoherent, twisting my hands.

Let me offer another version. Earlier that winter, I had become fascinated with, terrified by, signs of plenty all around me. My meals were discreetly whittled down to nothing. I became a very sloppy eater; large mouthfuls fell from me everywhere. I lovingly chewed on air, lingered compulsively over shadowy meals. I learned to tell lies by the dainty fistful. I dirtied plates with food I fed to my dog and left them conspicuously in the sink. I began to shake with cold in the full sunlight, to lie awake all night — a teenage insomniac — and to sag under the effort it took to drive a wedge between myself and the world. In short, within three months, I was able to stand, starved, proudly hobbled, and say, "Here! Here is all that I am not!" Thus I learned late-twentieth-century love — I came to love bone and hollow, shadow and shoulder wing. And I wouldn't let anyone touch me.

But the sparkling-eyed boy was none of these things. He was the plenty that allows such love. (That is, we wouldn't survive if everyone waned and no one waxed.) No — that's not right. He was the plenty and the hungry stare that imagined that I might sate him.

So perhaps I came to love the sparkling-eyed boy because otherwise I might have fallen into a clatter of bones. And the rest is true: I came back from Canada, restless to be filled out with the shadow of the boy. Only, for the first time in many years, he did not come racing down my road.

But what have I done? If I have offered up my own desire as a symptom of starvation, can I honestly still offer the desire of the boy as desire unmitigatedly for *me*? Sometimes I worry that I have painted a picture of the sparkling-eyed boy surrounded by sturdy pines: natural man, an Adam untouched by the myths of brutality of human love, gazing naively on an Eve uncontrollably sullied by her historical moment. There we were, standing on opposite sides of the garden, me with the pulp of apple along my gums, him with a rumbling stomach.

My god, there are so many myths to sort through and discard. This picture is all wrong! I was not that Eve; he was not that Adam. You see, the sparkling-eyed boy was in the rather startling—and emasculating—position of lacking a mother. Not even the thickest clots of forest, the most expansive gestures of water, can keep me from putting Freud into play.

She had run off with another man a few years before and left a husband, a college-bound daughter, and a boy on the cusp of adolescence. These three were left in a small house in a town with only a bar/general store, a post office, and a gas station/bait store. All I can think now is how can a boy become a man while pining mortally for a mother who has not chosen him above all other earthly things? If those of us around him who called ourselves "friend" had been able blindly to grope the shapes of bereavement in his face with literate fingers, we would not have been surprised if the face of the sparkling-eyed boy told us terrible things.

It's shocking to the ego to think of us this way, but what if he had already rehearsed the role of male pining for inaccessible, all-important female before he cast me in the drama?

● ● ●

I'm killing all of the romance here. I'll try again.

Water is the great reflector. It can mirror the elusive cloud back to itself so that, frankly, it understands itself better than before. So when the sparkling-eyed boy didn't come to me that summer, I did what I always do when my heart would drag me to the bottom if it got the chance. I consulted the water.

Despite its hypnotic dappling, its endless enthusiasm for making the same wave over and over, water seems to say, "I would make an even bigger noise when I hit the shore if I could." So, if the sparkling-eyed boy wasn't now coming to me, I would have to go to him. I sent a message through one of his friends—a sort of presumptuous I'm-ready-for-you-now message. I was not, as you can imagine, versed in the proper etiquette for wooing anyone. I had no sense that he might have a life of his own that I might be disrupting, or that I would not be eternally attractive to him. I couldn't imagine him as a fully etched human being, angry at my assumptions. I can imagine that now, but then I told this friend of his that I liked him in "that way." And he sent me a letter.

I kept it. It's dated July 11, 1988, and it was stamped and mailed to me even though he lived not three miles away. He says he's lying in bed in the middle of the night, writing the letter. (I'm sure I had never imagined a boy alone in that quiet, wide-open time of night, shirtless and propped up over a notebook. I thought quiet was the province of girls, who, it seemed to me, had more cause for sleeplessness. But he gave me this image of himself, alone, the buzz of the day extinguished.) He tells me what I'd known—that he's "liked me very much" for a long time. Then he chides me, tells me he thought he knew me until I refused him. (He was instinctively clever: When someone says he knows you and your actions have betrayed your true self, who are you to argue? I couldn't resist someone who both knew *and* wanted me.) He said, in adolescent dramatics, that he "almost died." I'd made him accept what he didn't want to. (All of the moments of warmth between us made him trust his emotions to me, moments alone with him when we didn't have to pretend anything for anyone — riding in his car, laughing and fussing over the tape deck; throwing the stick for my dog until her gums bled. I wonder about all of the moments that made his father trust his mother.) He said he didn't know where to start with me, so he was writing this letter, telling me he would "give it a try."

In the part of the letter that says the most, though, he writes about the weeklong trip to Florida he's about to take with his cousin the next day. He says he wishes he could spend that time with me, but that he's "never been anywhere before" so he's still going. I think, now, of an eighteen-year-old who has been almost nowhere outside of the U.P., yearning to go to Florida because it's *somewhere*. This statement seems to loom over our lives: he's never been *anywhere* before, and Florida is *somewhere*.

I suppose, god help me, that at the time I thought it was a vaguely dissatisfying love letter. Though I read it now in its full poignancy: as a portrait of a boy confused, earnest, longing for experience and love, a bit angry I had made him wait so long, fully cognizant of what he might be lacking and of the difficult choices that lay ahead of him. But at the time I wanted more devotion, more superlatives, more power. I wanted to take his strength as my own. When did I read it correctly? Or am I still not getting it right?

He went to Florida. And when he returned a week later, we started "going out." I went to his baseball games; we went to the beach; he came down and played cards with my mom and me as he'd always done; we argued about music; I helped him bale hay and work on building his father's house — I still have the scar on my knee from when I slid down the shingles of the roof. We kissed and rolled around a bit. We lay on his bed — I'd never lain with a boy on a bed before — and whispered to each other. He told me what he'd done in the past and with whom. I

told him I hadn't done it yet and no one had even . . . you know
. . . touched me on the bra. I don't know if he believed me.
Though we never removed one article of clothing, I felt thin
and right against his chest.

But then something remarkable happened. With a month of
summer left, he stopped coming to see me. He just dropped out
of my life. The first time I knew something was wrong was
when he didn't show up to take me home from the job I'd gotten washing dishes at the local bar/restaurant. I was shaking
from my dinner of coffee and Sweet'N Low. I sat in the parking
lot, swatting mosquitoes and nursing my pruned hands, but he
never came, and it seemed to me that growing up was merely
the process of becoming more and more damaged.

I did nothing. I had no more wooing left in me — my soul
was not generous; it was even thinner than I was. Gradually, I
became a specter. The starvation wasn't logical. There didn't
seem to be any reason why it had started in the first place, and
losing the sparkling-eyed boy didn't escalate it. Though scant-
ily, I *was* eating. But I was haunting the countryside. I spent my
days alone. My sister, barely able to tolerate any of us, hadn't
returned from college. My dad, afraid of losing his drafting job,
martyred himself alone in Detroit. And my mother, up north
with me, enjoyed her first breath of freedom, one from which
she wouldn't be able to return. At the end of the summer, she
would tell my sister and me that she would be leaving my
father. Even in the moment, though, I knew somehow that
skeins wound for years were unraveling. My ballast was gone,
and for a good part of every day I drove my mother's car, weav-
ing around on the back roads, allowing myself a few times a
week to pass by the sparkling-eyed boy's house or the construction site where I thought he might be working that day. I never
saw him, though. Mostly I just hoped I would get lost on some
of the barely marked roads through the woods and the old
fields homesteaders had abandoned long ago. I was reduced

to a pale jumble of hurt with sprayed hair in a maroon Olds-
mobile.

I began every once in a while to pull over and pick wildflowers along the side of the road or deep in the fields. And perhaps,
even though I was a deeply ridiculous character, a character
L. M. Montgomery might be proud of—a girl alone in nature,
plucking flowers, sighing, on the verge of poetry—for the first
time in my life I was acting without any hope of cutting a romantic figure. I hoped, in fact, that I was invisible. Audienceless.
It was embarrassing, toting home armload after armload of
wildflowers because that was all I could think to do with myself.
The deep velvet car seats were stained with their pollen. I guess
I was, though I could never admit it, heartbroken over the sparkling-eyed boy. When nothing around me was fecund—not my
body, not my family, not my love with the sparkling-eyed boy, I
turned to the earth and gathered up its most extravagant
bounty, its riotous sex. The flowers bloomed with vigor, without shame, calling the world to them.

I didn't see him again until the end of the summer at the an-
nual Fireman's Day picnic and dance. That night at the dance,
he walked into the Township Hall with a few of his friends, and,
as he passed me, he pinched the skin of my back and said,
"Ooooh, I think you're getting fat." It's so unfair that we live
what we don't understand, and then understand when we can
no longer live it. I didn't hear the fear in his voice, the anger that
was fear that was love in the sharp end of his fingertips. I was
dizzy with anger and shame: either he was mocking me or he
really did think I was fat. He was cruel, a million miles away, I
thought. We didn't speak the rest of the night, and then I went
home for my senior year.

But that's not how things ended finally between us. My parents
and I drove up to the U.P. the next Memorial Day weekend.
(Though they were separating, she was still taking care of

him.) I told myself I was long past mourning—I didn't care about him or the dissolution of my parents' marriage or my sister's distance. I had a trip to England planned for later that summer, and then college with my best friend, and huge, unwieldy dreams that didn't include even one heartache. I was in control again, breezy and unflinching. I wanted people to know I could go anywhere, do anything. And when I saw him at a community center dance on Saturday night, I was a chiseled ice sculpture of a girl. The light went right through me; I reflected nothing back to him. But I grinned and sparkled at other people I knew until I left proudly alone without looking back. But he caught up with me in the parking lot.

"Amy," he said, "wait up a minute. Please."

I paused, looking at him silently, one eyebrow arched nearly to my hairline.

"I know you probably don't want to talk to me, but can we, I don't know, just take a ride?" He was intense and shuffling at the same time.

Precipice. Who was watching? What would my future say about this moment?

"I don't know, ——. I don't think we have anything to talk about."

"Please. Let's just go for a drive." Was this the old supplicant? I'm shamed to say I needed this, needed to imagine myself loved more than I loved. I still do. I agreed stiffly and we rode for a long time in the cab of his pickup truck without speaking. When I sighed loudly and said I should get back, he pulled onto a dirt road and parked the truck.

He stared out over his hands on the steering wheel. A full year of drywalling had cut itself into his knuckles and the cast of his mouth. The woods were absolutely black, and their quiet was on the edge of a scream. "I'm so sorry about last summer," he said.

"Sorry for what? There's nothing to be sorry about."

"You know. I'm sorry for acting the way I did. For not coming to see you."

"Oh, that's no big deal. We're all free to do what we want to do. It didn't matter one way or the other." I could tell I was hurting him. He wasn't sure whether to believe my nonchalance or not. And I wasn't sure I wanted him to. He might give up. He might let me go and not make me feel things. Part of me wanted to be driving home to the cabin alone, safe, triumphant. I wonder what the different parts of him wanted.

He pressed on, braver for his fear: "It's just that you were so skinny and you wouldn't eat around me and . . . I didn't know what to do."

For a moment I was stunned outside of myself. I saw a flash of a scene from the previous summer: We were at the beach under full sunlight but I was covered in goose bumps, quiet, sad, unable to hear him for the din of suspicion and the constant tally of calories in my head. I never imagined that these things showed. Could a boy really have cared about my health, my mind? Then I said, with more honesty and insight (and frankly, more words) than I had thought myself capable of, "But we were friends. We were always good friends. And then, I was sick and needed you. And you ran away. What kind of friend is that?"

"You're right. I screwed up." We were both crying now. "Can I have another chance? Can we try again?" Didn't he know that I should apologize, too? For always making him be braver and truer?

We were kissing and crying and I felt that with this talk we had just grown up together even though it lasted all of two minutes and we were still children. And with this gesture — our hands in each other's hair, foreheads pressed together — we were finally home, balanced precariously against each other. But we had already lost our moment. Even though we had one more summer together, I was already protecting myself, knowing I would soon be elsewhere. And he? He was already protecting himself, knowing he would let me go.

When Have We Not Been Weak, Summer 1999

The glass of ice water he has given me is sweating between my knees. I am sitting next to him on his couch. My friend sits in a chair nearby. Just beyond his head, I can see the outline of a baby swing.

"I guess men," he says, "just like sex a lot."

My face is frozen in a smile. The sparkling-eyed boy, who never would have even alluded to the word *sex* in front of me ten years ago, is making sweeping statements about it. He must find comfort in the easy cliché: men want sex; women want . . . what? China sets, babies, good recipes? Behind my frozen grin, I think, I could tell you stories, sparkling-eyed boy, that would cross your eyes. When, I wonder, have men ever liked sex more than women? But I play along because I am there and his wife is not and I want to know how I can be better than she is. Is it palpable? A sort of *I*-wouldn't-have-done-you-that-way tilt to my head? A nod that implies, You would have gotten everything with me, baby — Madonna, whore, Donna Reed, Joan of Arc, Marilyn Monroe, Leona Helmsley, JonBenet Ramsey, Yoko Ono, Tonya Harding, Golda Meir, Barbie, Martina Navratilova, Bessie Smith? Which one does he want from me tonight?

Later, I think he winks at me. We are talking about anything to avoid saying something that really matters or admitting that we have nothing to say or realizing that it is long past the point when my friend and I should have left. He is telling us that after I left him he took up competitive archery. To give a sense of the scope, he raises a circled finger and thumb to his eye and then he turns it toward me and—I think I see this—winks. He slowly lowers one fringed lid over a sparkling eye and continues to look at me, never missing a beat in his story. His other hand is resting on a pillow between us cross-stitched with the command "Bless This House." When he gets up to go to the bathroom, I turn the pillow face-down. I picture the bedroom upstairs, the sparkling-eyed boy and his wife rolled to opposite sides of a wide bed. The mere touch of the blankets makes him ache, and he trembles silently, adrift in the darkness.

Still later, not long before we must finally leave (it is, after all, close to two-thirty in the morning), we stand in the kitchen as he refills our water glasses. Only, when he hands the glass to me, his fingers touch mine longer, I think, than they need to. My head swims, and again I am frozen, able neither to cover his fingers with mine nor pull my hand away.

I admit, I am elated. I came to his house knowing nothing, not having had an unguarded moment with him for ten years; and I leave his house knowing that, whatever else has happened in those ten years, the sparkling-eyed boy has not completely forgotten me. He seems to be sending me signals. What signals? That he is sad, that he is lonely in his marriage, that he misses me?

It occurs to me several days later in a dizzying moment that I could be misreading the signal. What if he's not sad? What if they don't sleep at the edges of their bed but in the middle, in an indistinguishable lump? What if—really—what if he's thought of me only once, twice, over the years and that the whole night—the talk about sex, the wink, the press of his fingers — happened only because I was there and his wife was not, and because I *let* him?

Does he hold me lightly in his mind — as a whim, a joke, an ember to blow on and then mock its ready blush? Did he rest easily that night and say truthfully on the phone to his wife the next morning that "nothing much" was happening? Did he fail to commit the nuances of my face, the moments of possibility in my glance to memory, while I, months later, am writing this all down?

To him I am certainly not the name he can't bear to hear on anyone else's lips. I am not a fever that gets under his skin and makes him restless and sweaty in the clutch of winter. I am not, as I had secretly hoped, the love of his life. Why else would he have winked at me, baby pictures on the coffee table, a sweating glass between my knees?

An Aside About Sex

Whatever you're thinking, whatever evidence to the contrary, this book is not about sex.

I remember fighting on the phone when I was maybe nine or ten with the girl who lived across the street from us in Detroit, the girl my sister and I vied for throughout elementary school. I don't remember what I'd done, but she yelled at me, said I was schizophrenic and I needed help. Though she was probably just throwing out a word she'd heard somewhere, I was shocked at what I thought was her clairvoyance. I was so changeable, I was a danger to myself, to others. She had seen through me. I thought I knew what she meant—that I was a different person to every person. That I tried to carefully control my image, make myself what I thought someone needed me to be in the moment. I have been, all of my life, a private person, secretive even, consulting a baroque manual to see what's safe to say or do. This one might like me if she knows this snippet but not that one; he will smirk at this gesture but grin at that. Though I have said too much already, I want you to see me as unassailable. So let me get close, because I want to tell you and I want you to believe that this is not about sex, none of it. There are things at stake here for which sex is a poor substitute, and I am whispering this in your ear.

When do we have sex? When we're happy, sad? When we can turn our bedrooms into a stage? When our hormones lead us to it almost entirely of their own accord? When we feel that the noises of our bodies, the texture of our arches and thrusts, are too precious to escape the notice of another? When we are bored and can't think of a good reason to say no? When we are trying to prove to ourselves that we are, in fact, beautiful, powerful, alive; or, conversely, bruised, careless, and expendable? When we find someone with whom, for whatever reason, we are willing to take the greatest risk: the risk of realizing mid-act that he or she is not *it*. You may love this person so that you daily weep with adoration; still, he or she will never be the real object of sex. The real object is a nonobject. No matter the position we take, we will never possess what we desire. We will never even embody it, because what we desire is something beyond our skins, beyond the skins of our partners. And since we take this risk, we must also be ready to hate them — in fact, we must already hate them just a little bit so that we might someday discard them — saying, You, you have failed to make me happy, failed to make me rise above myself for more than a moment at a time — and then forget our own failures, our inability to make our moans give noise to every feeling for which sex is a substitute.

And just as we are disappointed, so must we disappoint. We should be sleepless with the fear of laying our fingers — however briefly, slightly — on the tender spot, the intersection of every fiber that tells people who they want to be. We should, none of us, have this power. As our bodies know nothing but decay, so our desires are malignant — they cannot hover, feather-light, around such sacred spots; we sink heavily, we press down our thumbs in their opposable brutality.

I'm suggesting that, evolutionarily speaking, sex for humans has become (beyond its peripheral reproductive function), roughly, only the response to some mixture of sadness, joy, love, anger, impatience, ambition, and melancholia bubbling over. Can an action, an embodiment, truly be a metaphor? Certainly, think of a salute, a wink, a hand slamming a door. But this particular action falls prey to the same foibles and failings as any tuft of words: imprecision, opacity, double entendre. In fact, sex is not even a metaphor—it is merely a simile. It is endlessly "like" something, "as if" something else. For me, almost three years completely single, heading into my thirties, teaching in a small town, sex with anyone, really, would be both too much and not enough. It doesn't seem worth the enormous risks. I would like to say this is what it's like to be single, but I think this is just what it's like to *be* when every gesture risks untold losses. My biggest fear is choosing wrongly and having regrets from which I cannot recover. Everything is very, very heavy when you're alone and ponderous and wary and you don't know anymore whom to please or how to do it.

Of course, I fear that I may have gone off—turned rancid like a bottle of olive oil. Imagine, if you will, the genes of a hyena perishing because the act of sex itself could not adequately embody the desire behind it, and the partner of the sex act could not be expected to be responsible for such inspiration. Imagine the hyena paralyzed, abstinent, plagued by visions of passionate kisses, unable to follow up on her momentary impulses. She pours her excess energies into activities for which she will not be remembered—oil paintings of sunsets, long walks through the desiccated grasses. I will, perhaps, think differently about sex someday. It is only a matter of time before I trade in one idealization for another. For can one actually have sex and not want to believe in it, however briefly? But for now, I will have friends and not lovers. I will idealize the *almost* of love, passion, envy, respect, the longings more exquisite for their inertia.

I am never far from the sparkling-eyed boy when speaking of these things. I am well aware that, whatever else he may be, the sparkling-eyed boy is still eighteen and the lover I will not let myself have. I conjure his dear, distant self preserved in the glow of an arrested summer sun that has the power neither to warm nor irritate me, his self that I cannot disappoint and with whom I cannot be disappointed, the perfect elsewhere on which I might dwell.

I can hardly believe what I've said already, not knowing how to please you. Yet I can tell you this because it is so innocent. Who is harmed? To what could anyone object? I was wrong about the greatest risk. It is not disillusionment or regret. The greatest risk is being known, fully, by anyone else. Which will not happen.

Ethics of Nonfiction

Don't be my friend. Don't tell me what you might fear, what you really think about your sister, how you got those bruises. Don't tell me anything. Don't even come by my house and laugh with your mouth open. I will count your fillings and know what you find funny. People who have very little to say for themselves are careless with the lives of others. I am a spiller of secrets — they plash easily out the sides of my mouth.

Writers have no ethics, if by ethics you mean respect for the lives and truths of others, and if by respect you mean leaving them alone, and if by leaving them alone you mean not ever seeing them as material. Words are a currency and the lives of others an entire economy. How much to tell? How shall it be told? What you know of someone else's life has one value when kept to yourself and a different value when told. One power when you shut the door behind you, lean in close to my ear, when we go to the movies together, laugh behind cinder-block buildings, send notes to each other from our own pens in our own hands. When I watch your face change like clouds moving over water. We feel so close, these intersections of our lives like a secret conduit. We actually believe we might feel the same way about something.

And then there is the power of turning your sigh into a metaphor, our car trip into a narrative with a significant ending. The power of turning you out of the inner folds of my life and into dialogue.

That time when we were kids and your father yelled at you in front of me and you didn't guard your face, which crumpled, as we would never want our faces to crumple, into the folds of an old man who knows for sure it won't get any better. I saw that. It was mine. And you knew I saw it, so it was ours. And now it is not.

We all want to be loved, but some of us are willing to gut our lives of secrets, their moist insides stiffening and cracking in the sun, then look, like a dog, for approval. Some of us are willing never to live a moment again until we've inked it on the page. Some of us don't know how else to live. I don't know how else to live. So don't be my friend.

PART IV

Our Lives — with a Lead and a Hook and a Close

Dearest Boy,

(Take 2)

Smoke and water, the burning of old wood. I've kept this night to myself so far. It's as if just because the sky was smeared with a red-gold paste, I remember that scene more clearly than most events of my youth. A barn was on fire. Do you remember? Were you there? It was just a half mile from my cabin, on a hill overlooking the bay. I have told stories that made you the mute and muddy hero of that night, pumping water from the volunteer fire truck long after hope for the barn. I can see you, happy because you had something important to do, stricken light washing across your body. But I have lied in worse ways, I suppose. When is a story a lie? When it forgets to leave something human and difficult at its core.

I had never seen anything burn uncontained before, and at that moment I felt time slide sideways, as if I were allowed to feel other, older moments within this moment combusting in front of me. Every time I've described this night before, I've had to invent something more dramatic to try to convey the experience: efforts to save the barn, love among the firemen, a trapped cow—god help me. It was just a leaning barn used for winter hay, but the scene didn't need embellishing. The truth is, the sight of that barn on fire thrilled me through every last neuron: the tremendous spitting roar, the orange light rippling across our faces, making us look like fanatics. The air around our circled bodies was thick with smoke and the smell of fear. Something missing had returned for just a moment — the threat of death.

I like to remember that night as if you were there, as if you understood me. But, honestly, I don't remember seeing you. I don't even remember how old I was or how I happened to be there to see it burning.

I must have looked around me, though. The faces in the small crowd must be my own memory and not a movie scene. They were beatific, orange, raised to the highest tongue of flame, as if it were a sign of the beginning of the end. Their backs were turned black with night. It was as if our lives in time-lapse photography were playing at high speed in front of us, as if our own skins were rippling with heat, as if the sun had actually set into the field and was reducing itself to ashes. In our pulse points we felt the tap of our meltable hearts. There is nothing more thrilling than looking at your own demise and finding it beautiful. Weren't you there? Wasn't it a gorgeous night?

Epistolary Evidence, Summer 1999

A few summers ago, the same night our fingers touched in the sweat around a glass of ice water, the letters slid into the conversation — another weighty lump between us — much as they had slid into his home again after many years. My best friend, my chaperone as it were, was on the porch smoking her last cigarette when the sparkling-eyed boy said casually: "A few days ago my dad cleaned out his basement and dropped a box of my things over here when I wasn't home. And apparently there were some old letters from girls in there. Some old letters from you. And, well, my wife got pretty upset."

"Letters?" I say, listening hard now to my breath in my own ears, as if I'm in deep space or under water and just breathing is a triumph.

"Yeah, letters from you. Well, she read them and, well, I was in for it when I got home."

"Letters? From me? Are you sure?"

"Yes. Old letters. From you."

"It's just . . . I don't remember writing any letters . . . except one . . . you know . . . a few years ago. I don't remember any letters." I can feel the pulse in my eardrum as if a tap on the inner chamber of a stranger.

"Well, do you remember going out? You know, we did go out for a while."

"Yes. I remember. Of course."

But I don't remember letters. Real words on pages, maybe dingy envelopes, misspelled words. The truth about the girl who wrote them, maybe about the boy who kept them. The part of me writing about the remnants of the sparkling-eyed boy and my own dumb, young self has been struck a walloping blow. No matter what, I think, we want a self that seems knowable at least to us, defensible. In moments like this, my self is a glass dropped I didn't know I was carrying—startled and broken all at once; it is impossible to tell how the pieces should fit together or even if they were mine in the first place or just stray bits swept in. I viciously *need* to know what a younger me might have written to a younger him, and when and why. I want to start breathing again and demand that he place the letters in my palm; I want, essentially, to say, Tell me about me, make me whole again. I need to *not* know that the kind of truth memory offers turns us irreparably into liars and cheats and strangers to others or ourselves.

The less dire part of me that enjoys a good joke, however, smiles at the uncomfortable irony of unrecalled letters—the writer who has utterly forgotten writing—and listens to the sparkling-eyed boy continue in the vein of "Jealousy."

I think later: We are made of so many silly, clever, pathetic, touching, sincere, or boring (mostly boring) pieces, of which we cannot keep track. Every once in a while someone is keeping track of them for us. Which is either a blessing or a curse—at any moment, by a number of people I could be reminded that I'm a moral coward, reminded of the enormous curly confection I made of my hair in tenth grade, reminded

how many times I've said I don't want, I don't need, a boyfriend.

I think later: When we speak, you and I, it means nothing—the
venting of a few signals across the tops of our brains. But what
about our brains' deep curls and valleys, what about the dark
areas on the CAT scans, and everything we've forgotten, the
promises made, letters sent, impressions given—all dropped
and lost. The effect is that I can't turn an evening's conversation
into a lifetime of knowing. And neither can you. The nature of
experience (the disconnect between the full force of our brains
and histories from our selves in a moment) won't let us.

I think later: He is apparently well loved in this life. To be that
loved in a marriage must be good, gratifying, filling.

I wonder even later, though, how my letters could have so
upset his wife (who has the rosiest baby, the permanent fusing
of his sperm and her egg). Was it simply that they still existed?
But, I tell myself, between my teeth a tiny kernel of bitterness,
the sparkling-eyed boy didn't keep the letters in a secret place
in his nightstand or, safer, in his garage workbench, wrapped in
a patterned paper that made his heart leap; they were forgotten
in a box in his father's basement. Was it something in the letters, then? Who could be troubled by the easily mocked words
of an eighteen-year-old girl? If I had sent something deeply in-
criminating even a decade later, what could it have been? We'd
never had sex, and I was wholly incapable of writing erotica at
the time. Something more subtle, perhaps? In my head is a
home movie of his boy's body flying from the county dock into
the bay, the froth swallowing him whole, wide-open eyes going
under. All of that untethered joy. She has from this time in his
life only two-dimensional pictures and his own version of him-

self. When we decide to take someone, say, a boy, for the rest of his life, we want every shining and lousy moment, not just the ones we happen to have been there for, but the tender, searching years before everything was settled. We want to have been predestined, locked into his red corpuscles since birth. But then there's a bundle of letters from the time his blood pounded free of us against the wall of his body.

I am so smug — accusing her when I have been equally possessive in my life, if not more so. Mustn't I admit to holding between my fingers old letters sent to my then-boyfriends by their ex-girlfriends, wondering if I had the courage to put them back unread where I'd found them. I read them, of course. I have memories of pages unfolding in my palm, weighty, saturated with meaning. I can even sense in the texture of the paper the fossil of his anticipation as he first opened it however long ago. My suspicion has always been that whatever pangs he felt then, with this other love, his heart might never precisely reproduce with me. I suppose, though, the root of this seemingly irrational jealousy is simply that the letters are evidence he has loved and been loved by others before me. This evidence makes it difficult to deny the ease with which I may myself become one of his others, or I might make him one of my others rather than my one. A bitter caveat to the mythology we must try to construct of our loves: anytime we begin again, with hope and enthusiasm and lovely, scribbled notes, we must admit to having begun before, and ended.

Still later, I wonder if he got a quiet moment with the letters when he didn't have to protect the expressions on his face. If not, did he want to?

Later that same summer, I sorted through boxes stored in *my* mother's basement, boxes I hadn't opened since she left my dad and moved into her own house at the end of my senior year of

high school. Among piles of old papers, I found two folded letters from him. I had remembered these notes but had not
imagined they still existed. If my life had taken a slightly different angle, would his letters still mean more than any of the
other letters I found with them? A love card with a poem from
a punker boy I'd waited tables with, kissed, and asked to my
senior prom just because he was strange, left roses on my
windshield, and didn't go to my high school. Or the postcard
from a girl I'd been friends with in high school but hadn't
treated very well. She killed herself sometime after college.
Why should his two shaky letters mean more than theirs? Our
brains must use an impenetrable algorithm to decide what gets
the force of our emotions and intellect. I know I felt a vague
sense of obligations unmet when I read the other letters, but I
felt a shock of luck and gratitude when I held this concrete evidence of the sparkling-eyed boy in my hands.

Loves that begin in letters are so different from loves that begin
with swimming together, playing cards, laughing at inanities.
With the latter, even if what you feel you might call love, when
the time comes to write a letter, say, when you are nine hours
away at college, you find you really have nothing to say, no way
to put yourself onto a piece of paper. In this way, I can't imagine what I wrote to him. Did I allow the pretensions I so desperately wanted to adopt to make it onto the page?

Sept. 5, 1989

Dear ——,

I've been marooned in a nearly landlocked state growing fields of the same corn stalk over and over with nauseat-
ing perseverance.

The distance from my dorm room to my classes is one

unit in my separation from trees as I know them. Here, in this state, trees stand in the middle of corn fields, occasional, or tightly clasped in panicked copses.

The water from the drinking fountain is, they tell me, occasionally toxic, clouded with nitrogen runoff. I drink it anyway, not having much of a choice. I remember great gulps of well water splashing down my throat, dripping from my cheeks and chin.

I have no reference here at all for the feeling of lake or river water rippling across all of me. If I know anything about myself, it's that I must negotiate the edges of things and must often be submerged. Thus I am very lonely, with not an edge in sight.

The stars are all wrong here. I wander around at night and lose my way where it would seem impossible to lose anything. That is, anything I wanted to lose. Do you grow impatient for a mention of yourself? Do you long to see your name circumscribed with hearts? I don't blame you — really I don't. I would wish for the same thing — and then some; I've always wanted more than I wanted to give. But if you are dissatisfied, you have misunderstood me. I have been speaking of you from the first word.

Love, Amy

P.S.: Have your short trips elsewhere taught you that your own green and blue corner — yes, quite literally, corner — of the world has a scent like no other? I know I can't describe it so I won't even try. But the evening that you find this in your mailbox, will you stand outside and breathe for me? I think you will know what I mean.

At that age, I couldn't have written a purplish, grand, or even expressive letter to anyone. I'm revealing more about what I want myself to have been than what I was: I would rather have been absurdly serious than empty. And though I have taken such liberties with the details of this boy and professed such love I'll never have to prove—in other words, though I owe him more than I could repay, I can't stand the thought of him having some small part of me I can't remember, imagine, or control. Letters are so vulgarly tangible! As if they are the only evidence we can trust of a moment, a mood, an entire relationship, a being. Damn it! What did I write, what did they read, how did they read it, how would I want them to read it?

Oct. 12, 1989

——!

How are you?! I know its been a while. Sorry. But there's just been so much to do to get settled in here after our trip this summer. My friend from high school and I had a really good time in the U.K.—a whole month—smashing, as they say! I know you thought it was silly to go, but it was a really good transition, you know, into college. We got some neat stuff there to decorate our dorm room. It's really tiny, as you can imagine—one room for the two of us. But we've put up some of the things we got and it looks pretty good. We're in an all-girl dorm—I hear they call it the "Virgin Vault." That should make you feel assured! Our neighbors violate the rules all the time, though. They only seem to care about drinking and finding guys. I think they know we're pretty disgusted with them.

Anyway, I've got tons of homework—I'm in mostly small classes and the amount of homework is large (calculus, chemistry, German, etc.). I have an Honors English class too, writing essays, and the guy who's teaching it—I think you'd hate him. He's very messy and he talks politics. He actually said the only reason he wouldn't do coke is because of how many people are killed bringing it into the

country. I can picture his apartment, all books, dishes, ciga-
rettes, maybe whiskey and pieces of paper. But I really like
him.

Gotta go — tons to do! Hope all is well in the North-
country, Amy

How did it end, the letter writing, our hold on each other, that
loyalty and gratitude for knowing each other through our most
difficult years? There is often no event by which people are lost
from us. We may have no red plot points for a graph. We might
point to a fight, a divorce paper, an unyielding "let's just be
friends"; but we know how many barely audible sighs precede
such moments, how many walks at night alone, how many
times his or her face seems like a caricature of the person we
loved. We realize they are no longer the extra skeleton in us
that keeps us from our own weakness. They lent us an organ or
two and our bodies have slowly rejected them. I've convicted
myself for leaving him, for letting him feel left, and yet I can't
remember how I did it. Memory has trouble with things that
aren't tight narratives. Which came first — story or the brain
that runs on story? How did I leave him?

Nov. 16, 1989

Dear ——,

This is a difficult letter for me to write . . . as evidenced
by my full wastebasket. I didn't realize it then, but when I
left there this summer, I must have had important questions (or, perhaps, doubts) about us. Where is it that we're
headed?

I say "we," but that pronoun conjures up a picture of us,
a fingertip away from each other in the clearest air, reflected in the clearest water. But you are there and I am
here and we don't know how to mention this distance.

When I think "you," I see the house that you are gutting and refinishing, I see you speaking to everyone — quick-tongued and glib, I see your sure and speedy fingers, I see your room with not one book in sight. When I think "me," I think of my friend and her exacting standards, I see films like Blue Velvet, I see me alone in foreign countries, I see the need to prove myself, endlessly. What, then, would happen to "you" if you were to leave that place? Could you ever be "you" again? And more and more, "I" am only what will happen in the future — that which I cannot predict.

But for some reason, what I remember most about being fifteen is playing cards with you as my partner. We cheated shamelessly, as you may recall, our eyes telling each other what we needed to know. I remember your sparkling, devilish looks that were meant for me alone. Tell me: Is this enough?

Love always, Amy

None of these is even close, I'm sure. I'm afraid I merely sent postcards from England — a picture of St. Paul's Cathedral with "London is great! . . . Lots of royalty buried and married here" scratched on the back. I'd worked for the trip all senior year, waitressing on the weekends until five a.m.; the sparkling-eyed boy said that going to England would be a waste of time. He wanted to spend the rest of the summer with me, as we had spent them for years now. He wanted July, August, to lie before him as the familiar idyll from which everyone had to wake come September, the idyll that allowed the coming of winter to crush only small bits of us — a thumb, shin, a bit of skin or hair — instead of the whole of us. But I didn't listen to him, of course. He wasn't right, of course. Not entirely. But if I had known how, I would have written: "Being around my friend makes me feel lonely sometimes; and she tries to make me feel stupid. You never make me feel lonely or stupid. But I need to be around people who make me feel stupid because that's the only way I can be sure they're terribly smart. And if they're terribly smart and they wouldn't be with just anyone, doesn't that make me smart, too? So you see, there's no chance for you, since you can't make me feel bad enough." I would add now: "But I will grow slowly out of this and I will regret the good souls I've looked through like windows on something better." I would add: "I could write you many letters now and remember every word." I would add: "Forgive my assumptions that you would want to read them. There is no end to my selfishness." I would add: "Forgive me for not remembering. Forgive me."

Blank

I'll bet the sparkling-eyed boy doesn't have the sort of frivolous paper fetish I have. He may round up scratch paper; but not hard-covered notebooks or stacks of medium-weight sheets he likes to run between his fingers. The way I remember it, he prefers wood in its less pulverized forms: trees, logs, planks. And a pen, when he wants it, is hard to find. There he is when the phone rings, fumbling with a message from the elementary school for his wife. He finds an old envelope and a black magic marker and squeaks out dramatic black letters. "Meeting on Wednesday" ends up looking like an omen on their kitchen table. He holds cartoonish construction pencils easily, but Bics slide through his fingers.

How does the sparkling-eyed boy fashion his thoughts? How does he react when he sees words strung across a page? Here is a mind so practical, so quick with jokes and agile with measurements, so different from my own that I doubt we would be able to entertain each other for long now. Musn't we write, I want to ask, in order to think, in order to give, to be? The answer is "No," apparently, "we musn't."

Even if he lacks the utensils to write, he loves words. When he is not working, he's talking, at any rate, so one can assume that he either loves words or needs them or both. In the city, people don't have to talk; the din of ubiquitous machine guts cancels their flapping tongues. But here, where the spaces between houses are many thousands of times larger than the houses themselves, speech is like a defense against an inhuman quiet. He tells strings of stories that usually end in laughter and shaking of heads all around. He knows his own stories; he knows the stories of his friends; he even knows the stories of the people who don't like him very much. He is a fine gossip, an old crone, an oral historian at heart. He needs stories to make light of the heft and sweat of work, to temper the stench and spill—the insufferably empty hours—of hunting, to convince us subtly that he is, after all, a good guy.

Words pour from his mouth in a stream, and yet he writes not one line. As far as I know, he has never had to look at the evidence of his thoughts in stacked rows of sense or nonsense and been sorry or proud or laid low. And he has never offered up a record of his own heart to those who must live without it. Speech lives only for a moment and then dissipates like a scent or the sound of a cough. How does he remember what has come before or solidify the ghosts of thought that slide through the hemispheres of his brain? Does he at least indulge himself in the pleasures of description? He could invent words for woods and their grains that would change the way we touch our coffee tables, that might make us sleep, stomachs down, on bare wood floors. But I have never heard him use these words.

Here is a piece of paper:

I rub it between my fingers, less aware of the paper than of my own fingerprints grating against it. Funny how I have never thought to describe paper as vulnerable. It can crumple, tear, smear, dissolve, and yet somehow it is I who am vulnerable before it. The paper would feel different between his fingers, I'm

sure, callused as they are. It would seem removed—just beyond the reach of feeling. Now between his fingers, the wide,
flat sides of the construction pencil, freshly sharpened with a
knife. This is how he makes his mark on it: short, quick whittles
to expose new lead.

If I could set the paper in front of him and ask him to string
words across it, what would he write? A list of supplies he
needs to get in —— tomorrow? A note to his wife asking her to
call her parents about when exactly they'll be visiting—and . . .
oh yes, he loves her? The lyrics of some song that's been tumbling about his head all day? A few wry sentences about how he
could write a lot better if he had gone to college like he wanted
to? Would he have even a few words for me?

Perhaps it is true that the only words we say are the words
we'd like to hear, that the praises we sing are the praises we
would delight in, that the faces we like are in some way our
own, that we touch our lovers in order to tell them how we
would like to be touched. This is how we spend our lives: looking for someone to get our stories straight, to read us as we
hope to be read and tell us all about it.

It's lonely never knowing a story, having no one to tell your
own. Maybe someday I'll hand the sparkling-eyed boy a thick
shuffle of these papers; but he will hand me nothing.

And yet what I have done with words to the smell of lake
water; to the sweet ache of my friendship with the sparkling-
eyed boy; to my father's better impulses, crushed; to my own
sadnesses, which might not seem so sad if I didn't dress them
and prop them up in a circle around me, sometimes makes me
sleepless with regret. I must say to myself: You have changed ir-
revocably your stories, his stories. You have misunderstood,
misrepresented, misspoken, misstepped, missed, missed. Leave
the sparkling-eyed boy alone. Spare the petrification of his
sinewy limbs, his healthy organs, glistening lungs, perfectly

taut kidneys, which you have no right to imagine, the impulses of his brain, which you will never rightly imagine. When you return this summer to visit, close your eyes as you pass his house set back near the woods. Pretend it is still a field of tall weeds and wildflowers untouched by human tool for a hundred years since the first settlers tried doggedly to farm the rock-choked soil. Imagine your adolescence without his russet head next to yours, the imprint of his gaze holding you up, his fingers teaching yours to bale hay. Imagine there is nothing he could write to you that you want to know.

Keep quiet and still.

Not another word.

Two Stories of Frustration, Summer 2000

I.

I have a stupid heart—though not stupider than most, I suppose—assiduously trained to string itself out on heartache; bereavement as a drug, satisfaction as a poison. I am a rock-and-roll cliché. Hell, I'm a country music cliché.

It is now Monday, and on Sunday I visited with the sparkling-eyed boy's best friend and his best friend's wife and new baby. It was a lovely visit. His wife was welcoming and mercifully loquacious. Their baby, milky white and dozy. They trusted me to hold it, touch its warm head. We drank beer from cold bottles; we parted friends. But the point is that he would have seen the sparkling-eyed boy today on the job. He undoubtedly would have told the sparkling-eyed boy that I had stopped by. Thus, I conclude, he might have stopped by our cabin on his way back from the construction site. Just to say hi, just to catch up. But it is seven-thirty and I have not yet heard the telltale crunch of gravel under the wheels of his truck. So I've walked a mile down the shore to the county boat launch, which has a cluster of benches looking out over the water. I have sought my mourning bench.

I can imagine him in his truck after work, his hands and

knees and shoulders habitually aching from rough use. He might absent-mindedly pick at a callus on his palms perfectly shaped to hold a hammer, level, sander. His neck must be salty, his T-shirt stained; he'd have only one hand on the wheel, fingers lifting in acknowledgment of passing drivers. He knows probably ninety percent of the drivers on the road, or they know him.

It's always this way: I can imagine every detail of his body — even those I've never seen — but the scaffolding of his brain, his decision-making process, stymie me. Of those people we lose, we lose their minds first: that is, our ability to predict how they might respond to anything, to place in order the things that they hold most dear, and to know how they have rewritten their own pasts. I don't know why he hasn't come to talk to me. Fear, anger, wisdom, indifference, the thought of his own baby waiting for him at home?

I would like to imagine that the water here forgives my melodrama drop by drop. And if I knew how to listen, the water might tell me, "I am deep and gray, ruffled by wind, and saturated with more sadness than you can imagine. Some I have brought on myself and some has been flung into me. Count yourself lucky that your eyes still flicker, that they can scan the opposite shoreline, or gauge the distance from wave to cloud, that your fingers can still curl into your palms, gouging them in anticipation of what will not come."

But, it must be clear, I am incapable of listening. I am thinking, Perhaps he'll come right now and I'm not there. Perhaps he's waiting to visit me tomorrow night, or the next, letting his anticipation expand inside his rib cage. Perhaps he remembers something about my voice he thought was special. Perhaps it has made him shy.

I get up and fall back into the narrow clutch of tree and shoreline, my own voice loud in my ears.

2.

I have a good friend (the only friend who has met the spar-kling-eyed boy) who is very smart and very difficult to fool. I call her up after three days at my father's tiny cabin, in the land of the sparkling-eyed boy. He still hasn't come, of course, and the silence of the gravel road is like a vacuum ready to suck my eardrums clean from my head.

"Help," I say. "I'm pining away to nothing for him. I'm so very sad." I am asking for her to work her miracles: putting my perspective into a better perspective. And also to not laugh at me — that I could be made sad by a boy right for me now in no way. The most taxing request, I'm sure.

"Well, it's not really about him, is it?" she says, getting warmed up.

"I know," I say. She offers a strong and bad-tasting medicine. Like a toddler, though I know how it's going to end, I turn my head to the side at the last minute: "No! I am at least partly pin-ing for *him*, for what is *objectively* the sparkling-eyed boy."

"Hmm," she says. "I believe that the affection, the nostalgia you hold for him is real, but the *pining*? You want some drama of the heart. You're pining for *something;* you're not really pin-ing for *him*."

"Yeah. But I wish I were."

[Laughter.]

Neither of us asks what I'm pining for. We don't have to. She's familiar with this language, too. We know I could be pin-ing to know that I can, to need something so badly I can be sure I'm alive. Because it feels good to feel bad sometimes. So much better than feeling nothing.

Her last words on the subject are "Remember, Amy. These are real lives here."

She means, among other things, his wife of seven years, his

baby born last November. She means I might not be the only one capable of manufacturing a romance. She means if he knew I was telling myself I needed him, he might think he needed me, too.

"Well, I'm not going to *do* anything," I say. I mean I'm not going to call him, drop by his house, corner him at his current construction site, ask him to tell me, tell me, tell me, tell me, tell me, tell me, tell me, tell me, tell me.

But she says, "Of course not" in a tone that implies I already have.

The Bodies of Preteen Boys
In Defense of Nostalgia

It is hard not to feel ridiculous writing, thinking about a twelve-year-old boy who doesn't even exist — at least not in the strictest sense. He is now a thirty-two-year-old man. Perhaps I should also feel a bit like a pervert, remembering his narrow limbs hauling him out of the water, how I could never look directly at the folds of the boys' bodies, their shoulder muscles swelling and tapering, their skin papering their bodies so closely. And I know very well I should feel like a soft-minded nostalgic, dwelling in these few memories of childhood. For all I know, the stuff of these memories might never have existed.

The cheesecloth of our minds is sometimes more like fishing net, only catching the largest, brightest, most struggling things; then we fill up a barrel, feed on it, and call that a life. And who knows what grows pike-sized? Some people forget whole marriages, whole vacations for which they saved for years, but remember the particular shade of teal of the miniature dump truck in which they hauled their small collection of plastic farm animals, remember it as well as their own mother's eye color. But what else besides our faulty memories do we have to tell us who we are? Our jobs, mates, houses, furniture, snapshots, etc? Let me tell you—and I didn't used to believe this—every single scrap of our magpie lives could disappear forever. Imagine your house and office burning down to soot, imagine the woman or man you call "home" retracting from your life like a glacier, and you have a start. We are left with only the freakish contents of our brains—our dreams that begin to seem like memories, and memories like dreams. And we are left with the short list of things our bodies can do and the long list of things our mouths can say. But that is all.

I remember the bodies of preteen boys, a whole twitching pack of them, but not in the way you might imagine—I wouldn't even have known how to picture the soft matter between their thighs. My sister and I met them the summer before she started high school and I started seventh grade, and they were a revelation. I knew boys at school. My friend and I decided weekly which of the four eligible boys in my class we would have a crush on. We even kept track in a notebook—a bloodless, businesslike affair in which the crushee never even looked at us. But up here, cut loose from our herds, we found a group of boys that were *our* boys. They didn't care if we wore the right brand of jeans—they didn't either. They didn't realize I was a geek. And we didn't know who they were in school or around these tiny towns.

We met almost every day to swim off the county dock, suddenly stripping off our mismatched T-shirts and shorts until we were down to thin layers of nylon and our prodding, jostling skin. No wonder our parents were worried. We were almost peeled down, like milkweed pods, to the thousands of seeds inside us.

Preteen love might be our first act of deep self-betrayal. We seem to gather up all of the things that have so far converged to create a self, drop them into a bay, and watch them bubble down through layers of limestone. In other words, we evict our own mind, should we even have one, then desire only what and whom we're supposed to desire. Or perhaps that was just me.

Of course the boy I settled on was in my sister's grade, tanned and muscled, with sun-bleached hair, mirrored shades, sleeveless shirts. He brought the Def Leppard tapes and the jam box. He drove his dad's ancient pickup with the other boys in the back. He was the coolly distant, sometimes funny, annoyed gravitational pull. I mutely worshiped him. But I wholly misunderstood boys. I thought boys might be like my father, I suppose, built for another century, admiring in women only perseverance, physical strength, quiet elegance, and devotion. I didn't know most boys looked for the girl who promised the most with her eyes and the strings of her bikini, her head thrown back in an imitation of confidence. The most suggestive thing I did was unhook one of the straps to my one-piece swimsuit in the water, pretend it was an accident, and then ask this golden boy to rehook it for me. I never showed him any of my goods, but I got four seconds of his fingers on the skin of my back, more if they fumbled.

I pulled this ruse more than once. Water from my suit and skin darkened the gravel around my feet. My thighs pushed together suffocatingly at the top, my back stiffly straight in the silence as hook searched for eye. Tick. Tick. After asking for his help, no other words sat in a worried lump between my teeth, no words pulsed down to a barricade at my tonsils, no words even congealed in the white space of my brain. I was play-acting and I didn't know my lines, but I hoped he'd find me *nobly* silent. And here is what gets me: It took years for me to wonder why I had nothing to say to him and most other boys. It took even longer for me to wonder what they had to say to me to make me laugh or think or admire them. I suppose back then I was a good animal, picking out the sturdiest, most admired, if dullest, mate. And I suppose right here and now I want more than that for the self I was then.

The sparkling-eyed boy was another species, but he was my species. He made faces, spoke in mocking voices, flailed his arms as he ran in circles around us. He was as silly and annoying and dramatic as I would have been if I'd let myself speak. Maybe he could tell, because he liked me from the start—he threw small stones at the ground near my feet, tried to throw me off the dock and beat me swimming back to its ladder; he made sure I was looking when he acrobated off the rickety platform someone had nailed into the dock years before. He knew no better than I did how to make someone like him. He annoyed the alpha male and he annoyed the alpha female, my sister; he didn't have a chance.

I'd never spent hot afternoons with boys before, their bodies stripped down to saturated swimsuits, so I can remember their thirteen-, fourteen-year-old bodies as if I'd made a study of them. But I insist that it was not lust that makes me remember the alpha male's smooth, caramel-colored skin, a layer of padding heralding softness to come, and the sparkling-eyed boy's tight, freckled skinniness, his limbs hanging loose and too long for his frame. (The alpha male would later play football; the sparkling-eyed boy, basketball.) I can see what they wore then—tube socks, jaggedly cut-off jeans, baseball jerseys. And how they held themselves—the alpha male at the end of the dock, elbows on his knees, slow complacency in his every curve; and the sparkling-eyed boy's constant movement in and out of the water like a narrow Labrador. His shirtless torso and paleish, hairy legs I remember most poignantly: they were vulnerable in their boyishness, but so starkly free of vanity, they were transcendent.

Yes, the sparkling-eyed boy's thirteen-year-old body—a body I did not desire at the time, a body that no longer exists—is precious to me. It was a child's body trembling at a crossroads, wanting to take on the sturdier powers of a man, not yet knowing he'd gain the needs of a man, too. There is something sad and permanent about the loss of a child's body into a predictable adult's. It's as if for a moment at that age the "way of all flesh" might be only a cynical rumor, as if puberty might have promised wings or tails, or violent colors, or otherworldly grace, and then stonily reneged. When I see him now, he is more than himself. He is still lean, but the twitching gangliness is buried under height, weight, experience, surfacing only in the restlessness of his mouth and the sad edges of his eyes. His body has been made to fulfill the narrow obligations of the life he has found himself leading. As has mine, yours. You see, and here it really is, we were at that point — all of us have been there — where we could have been anyone, could have decided the most curious things, drawn strange dialogue bubbles over our heads. But every day we had to shed possibilities like hundreds of baby teeth yanking free and scratching down our throats. And the adult teeth came in, real, immovable, carrying their own kernels of decay. We were twelve, thirteen, and we were already losing.

I had realized this a few years before, one night when my parents came in, first one, then the other, to say good night and a prayer. I loved them so fiercely at nine that my chest was crushed by this sudden wisdom that fell on me: I knew that I was growing up and that meant I was going inevitably to change and I would grow distant from my parents and they would no longer be the center of my world. I was so afraid of this premonition that over the next year I dragged all of my neglected dolls and stuffed animals from basement boxes and played with them with manufactured enthusiasm, trying not to monitor my genuineness; and I couldn't let my parents leave a room without a rib-cracking hug from me. But I knew I was only acting with Joycie, Barry, Dressy Bessy; just as I knew that the smiles I turned on my parents were mixed with a pity at their inevitable loss of me.

Can you pinpoint that moment? When you made a choice before you even knew that choosing was possible, or the terrifying nature of choices? You made a choice that seems ominous now — the flattening of a globe to a map, the map whittling down to directions on the back of a napkin, to one single street sign you've stolen and nailed to your wall. You made a choice that wasn't you, but it slowly became you. So here was one of those moments: I was eleven-almost-twelve, and my sister and I met our first locals up north. There were roughly five boys in front of me, and I had a choice. And even though the sparkling-eyed boy's heart vibrated through his every twitchy movement; even though his was a pained little soul open to me, legible; even though I could speak whole words to him, I chose the alpha male to moon silently over for years, as the sparkling-eyed boy chose to moon noisily over me. How can you take having a self seriously when it leads you so dramatically astray? It's true, we have to accept who we have become, but what is this thing I spend time with every day, this thing that is, in fact, "I," that is "you"? I realize the very question is passé or moot or childish, but doesn't it bother you? We could have been other selves, and we chose without any sense of the consequences. I chose a premade romantic model, I chose the option that would keep me from being chosen, I chose to be afraid of my own tongue, body, brain — and the choices stayed with me for years. What can I be now? What makes a self? What collection of selves did I bag up, weigh down, and toss into the St. Mary's River on those impossibly clear summer afternoons, so saturated with light and water and trees there was almost no room for us? I want to understand what I gave away and what I have left. I should feel lucky, I suppose, that we can even remember the taste of possibility, even if we don't get to swallow. But I am merely hungry, and I remember the look of the sparkling-eyed boy's ribs showing through his freckled skin. In those small fragments of memory, a lie I like to tell myself: we could have been so many things.

Inside-Out Days

Big Red over Bud Light formed the husk of his tongue. He offered it to me and I took it inside my mouth as if it were an honor to do so, as if we were being married in first the front seat and then the back. It was only my second kissing session, and I remember the sensations of the night — the beery cinnamon taste sudden in my mouth, the surprising gumminess of his skin. I *feel*, you understand, not just remember, the awkwardness of my body next to his, how my legs and elbows and neck had no idea how to turn themselves supple. He would remember nothing, I'm sure, of my dim freckles, arm hair, or wide-open eyes; this should make me angry, I suppose. He was quite drunk and I was sober, always sober. I had known only the soft, dry forearms of my mother and girlfriends, and his arms were nothing like theirs.

I was fifteen and he was the golden boy, not the sparkling-eyed boy. The details here are only shorthand to our shared experience. Conjure your first real crush, a crush so arduous it was like having a job — with heavy lifting, office gossip, and endless negotiating of nonexistent signs (Was that a longer-than-usual look my way? Did he play that song on purpose?). I had had a crush on him since I was twelve, but it had grown acute in the last year. In high school, more than 350 miles away,

I had been writing his initials, MIT, with a little mitten drawing in the top corner of every single notebook page. I'm sure I humiliated myself in other, less spectacular ways as well. I cried over him, of course, and I practiced my trumpet, shut in our little shower house behind the cabin, working myself into a romantic apex as I figured out how to play radio love songs, eyes streaming at the wobbly notes of love unreturned.

This is the boy who, on the Fourth of July, at the community center dance in the small town twenty miles down the road, asked me if I wanted to go to the car with him to get some gum. Big Red, to quicken the pulse.

I have always had trouble mastering lust for lust's sake—but I'm not boasting. I consider this a weakness. For me, lust has almost always had to mean something, to be justified. My need to be special has often overwhelmed other, savvier needs—for example, the need to read people appropriately or to learn from experience. If the boy I "loved," miracle of miracles, wanted me, some deep recognition must have passed between us, I reasoned. He must have spotted my elusive saving graces. Sometimes, I failed to realize, a boy just wants.

Later that night, my sister and someone else came out to drive us home. I sat in the back seat with the golden boy, pinned under the weight of his sleeping head. I was mortified to be the one people might talk about (*What did they do back there?* Not much, actually), but I was also proud. I had won something. I had been chosen, finally, as his special girl. And with him passed out on my shoulder, having kissed me and, rather lazily, I later realized, tried to feel me up, I was already the long-suffering girlfriend.

Since this story must seem familiar, you probably already know how it ends, but I'll tell you anyway. Two days later we all convened again on the dock for our swimming ritual, me sneaking looks at him, half-guilty memories of his foreign skin close at hand. I wondered what was supposed to happen next. How did people "go together," besides mingling spit in the back seats of cars? I could think of nothing to do with him beyond that night. After everyone else left, he asked me if he could give me a ride on his motorbike the quarter mile off the dock and around to the beginning of our family road.

Riding on the back of a motorcycle is clearly a prelude to sex — the full-body embrace, calves to cheek pressed against his back, his neck. No one doubts a man and a woman riding up to a restaurant together on a motorcycle are slamming roughly together morning and night. I've only been on a motorbike that once, but I knew even then it felt like the sex I hadn't yet had. To hang on for that brief ride, my inner thighs coated his outer thighs, my hands, water-chilled, molded his abdomen. I was restrained, though. It wasn't in me to disbelieve what everyone seemed to be saying: girls who give too much away give it all away, every bit of power they doubtfully had in the first place. A fucked girl, in other words, is fucked. So I rounded my shoulders and kept my breasts off his back. When I got off, I could still feel the press of him along my legs. Definitely sexier than the back seat of the car. Of course, this is when he dumps me.

Eyes on the gravel, usually placid hands suddenly agitated . . . *There's this girl I've been seeing on Drummond Island. I guess we've been sort of going out. So, I guess that's it. Just so you know.* And that was it.

He was just a boy, worth, perhaps, half a chapter. When my good friend happened to meet him years later, she couldn't believe he was the boy to whom I gave years of my earliest, purest crush; we were so incompatible. I should have been grateful to him, though. Maybe he seems a bastard, using me for my warm mouth and the scent of hair spray rubbed off at my neck — but he could have gone on using me. He might have later put

his hands under my sweater, guided my fist to his crotch, un-
clenched my fingers and rubbed them up and down; he might
have kneaded the muscles of my neck until they gave and then
pushed my face toward his open zipper. I might have reasoned
to myself: *Well . . . I've loved him for so long . . .* And I could have
continued to use him for a bewildering imitation of love. But
he didn't let that happen. He looked at my frozen face and told
me, *No.* Thank the gods for him, really.

I saw a shrink for a time, I'm not ashamed to say. I was desperate once in my life, had to fight the urge to step into traffic, lean
too far over the railing of a bridge over a New Jersey river. I pictured again and again pieces of my head spread on the wall behind the tiny futon that used to be my bed, a small, chill gun I
didn't own dropped to my lap. This is bad ethics: I shouldn't let
the people who will worry about me know this. What does it
serve to speak about those urges that have nothing to do with
making life more complex? Suicide is the ultimate simplifica-
tion, the rest from difficulty and industry. And shouldn't the
project of our lives be complexity? Doesn't this story locate
moments that bloom or fester with dis-ease? As children, we
learn the dimensions of the things around us in 2D. Then, in
adolescence, we learn those things all over again, in 3D. We
learn that, say, principles, rules, states of being, people, are re-
versible; that when you flip something inside out, you might
forget what it was a moment before, it is now so unlike itself.
Then, what we didn't want to know, the reverse of all of our
expectations, becomes tenacious memory.

Anyway, the doctor, my "lady," as I called her, once asked me
to remember experiences from my childhood in which I wit-
nessed anger. Oddly, it wasn't my father's frequent, slow-burn
pouting that came to mind. Nor my sister's whipcord insults,
her door slammed in my face. Nor was it, of course, my own
icy retreats. It was the face of my usually gentle, kind, and pa-

tient mother twisted up, her cheeks and eyes flushing red. Her
voice, when she finally got to me on the road (moments after
the golden boy had sputtered away) and grabbed my upper
arm until her fingers practically met through the skin, sounded
at once strangled, heartbroken, and (did I imagine it?) triumphant.

I was not abused; most people weren't. But I was — we all have
been — marked by fallible people, since there is no other kind.
And we do not learn democracy, if we learn it at all, from the
way we process experience. For what stays with us, perhaps
even defines us, are the anomalies, the irretrievable bad acts of
good people (not the habitual misdeeds of troubled people). It
is our own goodness that gives us the power to be terrible. I am
in my therapist's office learning to unmake the things that have
made me, and I remember my mother's rare anger first. The
reverse gesture. The star falling out of the sky. It seems hardly
fair that the best one of our family unit should be remembered
for the moment she fell through herself, through the careful
web of her own forbearance.

Imagine holding gauze to the skinless stomach and chest of a
man, picking stones and glass, bugs and the wheel of a Match-
box car out of the flesh below where the skin should be. Imagine working an ER and seeing women open like carrion, having
given their eyes and hearts and pancreases. Or the skulls of
men made liquid, the features of their faces turned inside out.
Motorcyclists all. My mother was a nurse, and what authority
she was denied elsewhere she wielded freely for the sake of our
health. She had told us many times, with eyes rolled up as if already seeing us without legs or scalp or teeth, never to ride a
motorcycle. But I hadn't thought "motorcycle" when I saw the
empty space on the back of the golden boy's meager dirt bike,
and the dirt road had been empty as always.

From where our private road begins, it curves along the shore about thirty yards, shielded by high grasses and raspberry brambles and saplings. It is usually a cool, quiet place unfolding to a short sequence of Bensons' cabins in various states of disrepair. For me, it has always held the promise of oasis, of the return home. But that day I had to walk back through images of my failure. I had been *used*, and there was nothing special in me. My mother, though, having watched me get on the motorbike, was waiting to show me just how special I was to her.

They were right — he was right, she was right. But they were terrible, too, coming at me in brutal succession, with both betrayal and shame, and I cried in the shower until my eyes swelled nearly shut. He might have told a prettier lie; she might have slowed her drive to my arm once she'd seen my fallen face.

Surprise — when you expect one thing and get another. The moment in which someone makes you see the richness of his or her potential, or reveals the way the world resists our imagined narratives. Churches would have us believe that faith is terribly difficult. It is not. We are built for belief, for blocking out contradiction, for the all-or-nothing, for trusting in only one aspect of a person or experience at a time. To resist the easy slide into death we must learn complexity, but it is difficult to remember — at all times — that everything is always also its opposite. Every romance has a bundle of tawdry motives; every act of love has a flesh-parting pinch. To remember the inside-out days and find them good takes everything we have. But it gives us even more. I am pathetic I am brave. You are narrow you are fervent. My mother is angry she is generous, grieved, doing the best she can.

If It Were to Happen, It Might Happen Like This

Absolute occurrence is irrelevant. A thing may happen and be a total lie; another thing may not happen and be truer than the truth.

—TIM O'BRIEN

❧

The Perfect Day

I imagine I have the perfect partner. She would be female; she would eat foods I hadn't yet heard of and know how to wear eye shadow. She would think I was clever or cute only when I wasn't trying to be, and she would teach me how to forgive. She would be lightly experienced in the ways of girls.

I lie next to her, this girlfriend of mine, the planes of her face portentous and moving. I hold her breast. It is such a soft bird — trembly but not at all scared to be held. Her stomach is talc. I watch my polished nails string bright spots through her hair, five small explosions in a field of brown. Have I really made her mouth curve so happily? I worship this woman as a man would — carefully, as if she were a delicate object; and I love her as a woman would — teasing out every strand of her she would wish to keep inside.

Mostly, I would want our courtship to be a happy movie montage of frenetic love — our days together as one long children's party with uncalled-for laughter, small cups of sweet, empty food, surprise gifts for everyone, the prettiest shoes, pink glasses with curlicue straws filled with vodka and something red, and music by which we run ourselves breathless. It is the happiest honor to make her laugh; I would play the clown for her for the rest of my life.

Our nights should be a cabaret—boys in boas and lipstick, girls in wigs and blush. Party frocks all around. So many glittering go-go boots, so many penciled-in moles. My wig is lilac and sprinkled with stars, and everyone gets the joke. I sway across the stage with rolling eyes and a finger to my dimple. Ha Ha Ha. Lovely drag queen, am I not? Her smile tells me that I am not, but I am the next best thing. In her pink and tasseled dress she is not even sure with whom she is flirting. She just twirls, flirt falling from her where it will. But the boys and girls and the boys and boys and the girls and girls here are more likely to swap lipsticks than kisses. The only reason for a clock is to tell when we have stayed up past four. And this is the best part of the night: lipstick trailing, hair askew, feet hurting too far from the ground, boys' chins darkening, girls shining through their powder. Through a drift of sequins, fans, tassels, dance cards, and curls from wigs of every color, we find each other. She sits on my lap, runs her finger down my nose, says, *What good jokes we have played, no? How everyone shone! How I want to take off your stockings and see you in the tenderness of your thighs.*

I tremble with every button she touches. She says love makes her fingers clumsy. I say I am shocked by the audacity of getting what I want. Yet even now, stripped to the essential strands of bone and vessel and nerve, even now I close my eyes to sleep and there is the sparkling-eyed boy—one dream subsuming another. A fantasy superior in every way simmers next to me in a sweet-smelling cloud, yet when my teenage love— so far away, so small and unfulfilled—appears to me, standing in the lake we have in common, crinkling his sparkly eyes and offering his hand, I take it and wade farther and farther under water, where he has no wife, where there are no intervening years. He says in perfect dream-speak, *There was no one to love but you. My heart would not have understood itself any other way.* I crush his fingers in my hand. He says, *I want to swim away with you, but you have to choose now or else I will kick and be gone, always gone.* I ask for more time, taking water into my lungs. He shakes his head, paddles his feet. He is drifting away, and I wake up, reaching out for him. I miss him as I would miss my own tongue.

She is still asleep, mouth parted as if mid-warning. I have always woken before the people around me into the blank space of morning. This is a dangerous hour. Our minds are not yet beholden to one another. I can think anything until she wakes. I think I might have laughed too loudly last night, danced like a fool, hoped for too much. I think: the shinier the joy, the thicker the tarnish. I am disappointed that I can still have thoughts like these, and I think there must be something I need yet. Must he take away my gold foil gift-when-everyone-else-has-forgotten; must she become one among others? May I not have an alpha *and* an omega? This is not his fault, but someone needs to be blamed for mornings withering before they start.

A Week at the Edge of the Woods
A Fictional Triptych of Adultery

I was raised to believe if you think a thing, you are as guilty as if you've done it.

I've been thinking: if I tempted him enough, he just might touch me. I don't believe he really would, but the thing about knowing someone since he was young is you think you can reach all of those vulnerable spots he has since learned to cover over. I'd lie to him and tell him, If I could do it all over again, everything would be different. I'd say he deserves the happiness only we could bring each other. That he has been giving and giving of himself, being good when other men would have been bad, for so long, he has earned this indiscretion. But this tactic doesn't need a special knowledge; it would work on many people, quick to believe themselves noble victims. We want to see in ourselves a special forbearance of a special burden. There is no room in this fantasy for evidence that feeling good doesn't require others to feel bad.

Earlier this summer, while visiting the sparkling-eyed boy and his wife with my father, they mentioned that she had taken their baby to visit her parents for a week earlier that summer. He had been alone for a week. I slowly turn his time "alone" into "lonely." I imagine we have done something with our bodies and I imagine that it needed to be done.

❧

I imagine it begins up north, of course, midsummer in his house by the edge of the woods. And this is how my fiction of our affair goes:

I convince myself before I park my car behind the barn, out of sight of the road, that I will just pop in and say hi, that this is our chance to catch up, listen with sympathy to each other's complaints. I laugh too much — I do this when I'm nervous. He talks animatedly in his frayed voice, perhaps testing the corners of his brain for his potential for adultery. I tell him a story, haltingly, about how I have these dreams about him — no, no (blush), not *those* kinds of dreams. Nice dreams, in which we walk together through the forest. We catch each other's eyes the moment we both are thinking: we did not plan this. We stand and walk to the stairs, and he stops on the landing, turns, and tucks a piece of hair behind my ear, a maternal gesture, as if to say, simultaneously, *Take comfort* and *Be ready*. Then he turns again, his feet rising before me with each step in clean white tube socks.

❧

The intimate talk of lovers we balance on each other's limbs, fragile as real English teacups. He is slow to lean into me. But one cannot step back in such moments. We have a template for most things: rising action, climax, denouement. For all stories we know well, there is no retreat — war, crop, conception, drug, affair. It is written: we must press closer before we part.

❧

He stands at the window, looking out at the purple-dark woods. In order to breathe into the moment peaceably, there are many things we must edit from our consciousness—drawers full of her clothes, the scent of apple room spray, the widening fissures of betrayal. Is he regretting what we have already done this first night? Is he listening to the sift of wind through the cedar and poplar? One could drift on that, buoyed by coyote and insect. Our room is dark, and so his form is thrown into relief (what a beautiful phrase, "thrown into relief," "catapulted into succor") by the light of the stars. His naked back is turned to me, his arm resting above his head against the sill. It looks as though he is being filled through his raised arm with molten body pooling and pressing at the edges of his long, work-formed shell. See? His lower half—legs and buttocks— have cooled already to a stark white; his upper half is still thick with churning liquid glowing brown under the surface. I understand, suddenly, the painter in love with his model, taking something, imparting something with his glance. Touch seems weak in comparison.

⌒

Here, in this bedroom, we do not fit into any representations of time: calendar, clock, television shows that switch on the hour or half hour, sundials, wheels of light and dark. But then time itself is only a quaint effort to make sense of living, as we, with our creased brows and careless sheets, are an effort to understand the nature of love. Love is, for the moment, an animal between us, breathing poorly as if from a wound.

This would be the great pleasure of an affair like this—the timelessness that purifies all things in its simplicity. In the imagined moment we two are so simple. Nothing will come of this, we would tell ourselves, no burdens of construction, of "we could be doing this wrong and the future will punish us."

And this is the great sadness—that without a future we are

essentially without a present, for we can give someone only so much now, and the rest is a promise of benefits to come. This, too, is a great sadness—that we will never be able to argue for our own goodness again.

Here is one remaining wish: I hope that someone will pull a pin so that we fall into sleep like hair tumbling from a bun.

I think he grows impatient with my laborious fingers. (Even in my imagination I am plodding in the moment.) They are nothing like his silvery digits. Surely he can do this better himself. Nothing about me is as quick as he is. Not my hands, not my skin, not my smile, my confidence, my eyes, and certainly not my tongue. I have always admired quick people because we value what we are not. I have lovingly watched the mouths and hands of the witty and agile, because these people control the present. I merely stand close, hoping to be implicated in the wit and movement by my mute presence.

The sparkling-eyed boy is agile and his skin is smooth just where it should be. Why has he allowed me here, spilled across his sheets, a collection of limbs and pregnant pauses? Maybe he likes my freckles; maybe he likes the scars on my knee; maybe he thinks I have something to give him. But it won't be words, I'm afraid. At least not yet. I have only the spaces between events and thoughts, between thoughts and the words that almost never come. You see, I have to go away, write words down and then bring them back. I'm waiting for someone to stick around and love me for that.

I imagine saying, "Bring your breath to my ear. I am sick of talking." He moves silently to where I sit on a maple dresser, my legs crossed in front of me. I watch where his leg attaches to his hip. It had seemed to me impossible that something so perfectly functional could still exist among humans. And yet here it is gliding toward me: a hip I love, a hip I want to either smash or deify, a hip that now bears bruises from my teeth. "Like this?" He covers my left ear with his mouth and slowly lets his warm air seep into me until I uncross my legs and circle them around those rolling hips. He can be dark when he wants to be. He looks around for the most uncomfortable spot in the room. There is a short flight of stairs by the door. We can take turns laying our backs across it, bruising in strips. He plucks me off the dresser and I cling to his upright body, trying to kiss him rather desperately with the whole of my mouth at once — tongue, teeth, gums. We are frantic against the wooden steps; we feel as if we're being cut to bits. He rolls me on top of him and I feel dirt sticking to my damp shoulders. I try to sit up but he holds my face close to his with two handfuls of hair. He is just breathing, but if he could he might say, "The rest of the world is gone, isn't it? Do you feel it anywhere?"

⌒

I saw a movie once in which a geisha and her lover become sexually obsessed with each other. They push and push each other into more and more dangerous territory, until, at the climax of both the movie and their relationship, she cinches a silk cord around his neck too tightly and strangles him. There is something of a Protestant ethic in this story: anything that's worth doing is worth doing right. That is, if you have not killed each other with your passion, it wasn't truly passion.

Even in my fiction, though, our passion ages:

I hold my arms around his rib cage, which expands and contracts as if it were something that could be broken open and set free from his spine, rhythmic like moth wings. I push my lips against his shoulder until the shudder of violence has passed through me and my fingernails, the heel of my hand, the sharp ends of my teeth, again can be trusted with his skin. We are dulled enough to be safe with each other after all.

⊸

I still dream of him regularly. But, since the birth of his daughter, the dreams have changed dramatically. Instead of both of us dropping effortlessly from the lives we've built into something earlier and seemingly elemental between us, the new dreams are guilt-hemmed. In them there is no question of his leaving his family, and so we are furtive, meeting for a quick exchange of words, sometimes a kiss. Often we are caught by someone — our faces in casts they wouldn't be if everything inside us were innocent. There's a softness to our expressions, an openness to our bodies turned slightly toward each other that gives us away. Then we usually scramble for propriety or excuses.

There are other stories in this fiction of our affair: he wants to know more about these dreams, the nice ones — he asks how often, what kinds. I can tell he thinks I'm obsessed with him, and a smile he can't help seeps across his face. I indulge him with as many distinct dreams as I can remember, demonstrating the at-long-last kiss repeatedly: You stand there and I stand here and then we lean toward each other, my cheek just brushing yours.

I would rather not recall a dream I actually had recently: There is a small crowd gathered for a football game he's playing in. I am down by the sidelines with him, as if I'm his girlfriend. I look up into the splintered bleachers and see his wife watching us, and, rather than slink away, I join her in the stands and commiserate about her husband's faults. Neither of us wants him at the end of our conversation.

⊸

A leaf limps across the gravel driveway, and I think at first it is a small animal. Can I help it? Everything is animal. Even the air smells furred and sinewed. It hangs, full of vesseled intent. A half an hour ago, I thought the fringe of my eyelashes was a bat flying across the room in search of a voluptuous fig. These mistakes are not problems of perception; they are gifts. Let us see animals wherever we look and let us read in them intention and passion and failure. Let us not believe that we are alone in this room, one species, sad and isolated, feeling that which crumbles in a moment and blows away—nothing out of something. No, the ceiling is thick with bats. I feel the pulsing of their hungry throats.

❧

Sometimes I think the emotions of an affair would be no more real than this fantasy—sooner or later something true and ugly would blast the film from the adulterer's eyes, after which passion, or even good humor, would take a monumental self-deception. I want to get this fiction right. What is the moment that would make the glamour of deceit or invention blister? I imagine that I, too, could be blasted by a scene like this:

Ten minutes ago, I couldn't imagine her. She wasn't real to me. Then I picked up the hairbrush lying on the dresser and saw several of her hairs wound around the bristles. They are longer than mine and a rich brown. I pull out a few and slide my fingertip up to the little white nodules at their base. I think about the tiny void in the follicles from which these hairs were tugged. I picture her sliding these bristles across her scalp, the private pleasure that must ripple outward down her neck, across her face. One small daily ritual. A piece of her body here in my hand. What else brings her pleasure? Cracking eggs over a stainless steel bowl. The first chilly September night she

needs the comforter. Fresh socks on her feet and her baby's ear-
lobe between her fingers.

When one takes somebody's husband, somebody's wife, all
one thinks about is oneself. That's it. If I'd had an affair with
the sparkling-eyed boy, I might have said that the worst part of
an affair has nothing to do with vows or propriety, that the
worst part is what you let yourself become, what you will be
unable to cease being. Unrepentantly monstrous in your selfishness. But, I would have been wrong. There's something
worse, and this conclusion would merely be further evidence
of my self-obsession. I would have called my actions many
other things — human, necessary, a historical arch completed. I
would have done anything not to see my ugliness. Look. See it.
See *her*.

⇔

He has almost never been the leaving one. I hope, if he ever left
this place, he'd feel as if he'd left his skin behind, dangling from
branch and rock and hanging in coils from his back like the
bark of a failing birch.

Affairs, by definition, end. And, so, I must imagine an end to
this one:

Before I go I tell him the one thing I've learned: When you leave
what has been your one and only place, you forever leave places.
You must concede an interchangeable sameness. When there is
no longer only one place, there are millions of dishearteningly
similar places. And, when there is no longer only one person,
there are millions of dishearteningly similar people. The flood-
gates of disillusionment open. The way I see it, he has struck a
bargain. To stay here he has had to forsake all of the other features of the world — and what he has, perhaps by default, loved
deeply was not enough to keep me here long ago.

We don't talk about it, but he must love her. They stay together, make things together, like a baby, like the visceral comfort of this house. Like promises. They must give each other moments of deepest relaxation when there is nothing else they need and no one else they'd like to be. If he loves me at all, it's because I leave.

❧

An affair (even this imagined one) is an aquarium of human experience, a controlled experiment with loving. The constant bubbles rising and breaking, neon castles, a bit of real kelp. When I finally leave the house, I lose not only love but the progress narrative that overlies our unions. We think: our actions must build to something. But he and I take nothing with us except a clutch of memories that will die when we die or probably sooner. We have been gasping at our own little bubbler, occasionally staring at our reflections in the glass. We are safe, but, dear fellow swimmer, this is a far cry from the ocean.

What does one do when one cannot go forward? When, in fact, there is no such thing as forward or backward or any other direction? Does one write another page and another until there is a neat stack that can be numbered one to ninety-three so that one may literally add up to something? Or does one remain a point forever rather than becoming a vector? I wish I could stop compulsively imagining myself with him. I wish I could sum up once and for all what I'm missing. I wish I could cull from myself that part of me that would never want to leave the sparkling-eyed boy, that could breathe sameness like air and never suffocate, that could love without doubting, and laugh without wounding, that would never, ever even think, "What the hell do you know? You've never even been to college!" This part of me would recline on this bed and gesture him toward me. It seems sometimes love is a hand held in the air for a moment, lightly moving. "Me? Do you mean me?" Yes, my darling, come over here. He would come and press his chest to my back, matching me length for length and spilling over at the head and feet like liquid.

↔

I have done this thing. With my mind.

I know there is a difference between the body and the mind. The body takes as its province the present, space, accountability. And crime. But I am more afraid, at times, of the province of the mind. Our thoughts alone can alienate us from our powers of self-defense. And what about you, in your many-storied lives? Would people guess that you only ask them what's wrong to get your turn to speak? Does your boyfriend know you imagine someone else as you slide your hand down his spine? This week is something I carry around in my mind, dangerous as powdered glass.

The Bath
A Simple Thing I Can Only Imagine

Years in the future, you bathe him at the end of the day, your legs molded around his, the parts of your body he finds mysterious, always mysterious, pressed around the small of his back. You squeeze water over his white thighs (they are almost translucent, like skim milk, not cream), ascend the peak of his knee with your sponge.

There is the love that speaks and then the love that washes. There is also, of course, the love that makes love. But at night, when it's over, there is no further you can go — you are just two skins facing each other, or curling, or touching back to back — two skins filled to the top. Not enough room inside for the entirety of another. What should you call intimacy, then? Can you get it with the lights on? Must you know the other's favorite song? Must both agree on the definition? Can you be alone? Must you see the other on the toilet? Must it include the worst thing that you feel inside or else you're lying? Is there any other way but the sharing of food? Must you see every season of the year together, put on your T-shirts, your sweaters, your overcoats, together? Can you have it once you know the scent of the other, which drifts unbidden from his or her skin and hair despite the salves we dab and sprinkle on? Could it be pushing your butterscotch into his mouth when he leans in for a kiss? Does it mean knowing more facts than anyone else: "I know that when you were twelve, you had a khaki parka that was mannish and ugly and made you cry on the inside but you wore it every day to school with a stiff, unglossed upper lip"? Must it require the damp nearness of time and space? If you imagine it's real, is it real?

Through your cheek and the corner of your mouth you can feel the heat of his back. Every day at the construction site the sun dements his cells, eggs them on to greater feats of darkness and spots. Above the waist he is deeply brown, and you are embracing a dying animal. Imagining the speed of malignant cell growth literally takes your breath away. At work he pounds, climbs, carries, measures, and burns, sometimes with a slight frown, sometimes with a grimace of nails, always unconcerned.

Just this morning you tried again with the sunblock. Your new tactic is a noble, puzzled, genuine indignation that he could love himself so little as to risk his own life. How could that be? you wonder aloud with a tilted head and moist, widening eyes. But he left without it, bare to the waist, driving away in his vulnerable, blameless skin. There is nothing between him and the sun.

If his freckles are lethal, though, you will take them on. There is room enough on your skin. What a stark canvas! And when that is full, they can cover the skin of your esophagus, your duodenum, that wettest, palest, cavity-dwelling skin. Your palms, the soles of your feet — wasted space! You have been careful enough with the sunblock for the both of you.

Is this intimacy?

. . .

It is not nobility or goodness. It is not love, precisely, this suggestion of biblical sacrifice and salvation.

You have stayed in the bath long enough for your skin to take on the wrinkled bloat of the drowned, and the bedroom is filled already with the stillness of his sleep. There is no one to tell you that you have had enough, it's time to get out. The water is cloudy, thicker on the surface. This must be intimacy, submersion in his sloughed cells, the dirt of his day.

There is the love that marries and the love that stays, your inevitable deaths the scaffolding around which you arrange your lives. You will watch his slow decay over the years, unable to do a thing. He will watch yours, inert. Surely this is intimacy, wearing the burden of two doomed bodies starting now.

PART V

The Final Days of Romanticism

Dearest Boy,
(Take 3)

I am afraid that people will see me as betraying my own kind: another story about a girl incomplete without a boy and his transformative love. But I hope that you understand: I don't want your seed, your ring, your paycheck, your security. I don't want to complain about work to you. I don't want you to drive when we go to the fish fry or throw your arm across my chest when you break for a deer. I don't want you to surprise me with flowers or plan an anniversary cruise to Alaska. I don't want to wake up next to you and tell you about that dream I had, ask you to scratch my back. I don't want to become frustrated with your taste in music or grow my hair long because you'd like to hold it in your hands and lay one strand, two strands, three strands across the bridge of your nose at night. I don't want ever to have to imagine the end of your imagination, my imagination, or feel, like a switchblade through my brain, the hope that yours is not the last body I'd like to be under, over, under again.

These things are fine in their own way — I mean that. But what I really want from you, and what you can expect from me, is to have my name scarred on your heart and yours on mine. So when we die, if they cut us open, they will know someone lived in us — me in you and you in me. Whatever that might mean.

Property Lines

I like to think of his property touching ours, a touch most legal and binding, and of roots crossing under the survey line and twisting around other roots or trees falling across from one side to the other. The business of living is no gentle affair, and no détente exists at property lines.

The sparkling-eyed boy rolls the humorless graph paper over the table. It is saturated with the air of an object well studied, adored. At this moment, as in other gestures of his most sincere effort, he belongs to a different age. Our generation is a generation of quitters. If we don't like something, we move on; if something becomes difficult, we scald it with irony. But he is like a root before me now, tenacious and digging, but prudent.

He points to uneven graphite lines with his last name on one side and mine on the other. He has been buying land behind his house in amounts that immediately bespeak loyalty and permanence in a place that can keep fewer than half of its young people. This place seems now only to sell its land to rich investors from the Lower Peninsula. The investors are hoping to make a killing when the eastern Upper Peninsula might someday become a tourist spot in earnest, or when it is the only scrap of wilderness left in the state. He is proud to show me his map, proud to come of age in this old-fashioned American way. I taste envy like the peel of a grapefruit in my mouth.

When I was a kid, I used to see the forest behind our cabins as boundless. I wasn't an idiot; I could work out the geography. But I'd step into the woods and the trees would leak into my brain and I would lose all sense that if I kept walking and walking, I'd eventually hit other houses, roads covered with asphalt. Perhaps it's the way forests refine our vision: we look only as high as the canopy lets us, our periphery is always framed by trunks. Our empirical brain kicks in — our eyes tell us all the world must be green and gray with leaf and trunk, fern and rock. Don't folktales warn us that there is something dangerous, disorienting about the woods? Our human powers falter there and we teeter into vertigo. We have left the highway and our houses of slaughtered trees and stepped into that which multiplies, multiplies, multiplies without us.

But here is a map drawn by county officials that clearly shows that the land is owned and the forest ends. Further, every acre is accounted for with last names printed along each side of the drawn lines. He retracts his hand from the map, and the light hairs of his forearm accidentally brush mine. We are looking at a representation of land, shrunk to the size of his kitchen table. Clearly, I knew other people owned parcels of this land, but I am suddenly forced to confront my illogical childhood sense that the land of the forest existed in some sort of prehistorical collective state. In one confused moment, I feel both the sharp, sudden splitting of the land into deeded chunks and the warmth of his tanned skin in illicit proximity.

The significance of his name next to mine on the map is elemental, mineral: we must share underground aquifers, there must be fossils with the same moment of expiration anchored on either side. As with an involuntary reflex, I hope he feels a secret satisfaction at his land leaning into my land, and mine leaning back, the great weight of us underground. His wife is here, talking to my father. She's not from here. She came from a relatively more populated area in a different state to take a job teaching at the local school. She never wanted to stay, but she married him and this is his home. I want to say, leaning over the map — not being local, she couldn't understand us. But I'm not from here either, and did I ever really intend to stay, to earn a right also to call this place home? Could he and I really speak so as to understand each other like natives?

In *Second Treatise on Government,* John Locke had a radical idea for a seventeenth-century Englishman. He thought that, ideally, you should only be able to acquire the right of ownership of land through your own physical exertions over it. What's more, you should have rights over only the land that you can, unaided, tend. This proposition, of course, gets complicated in the industrial age, more so in the postindustrial age, but in his own time, when the vast majority physically worked land belonging to a tiny minority, the suggestion was rather staggering. An idea at its heart utilitarian. And hopeful. What faith he must have had in the goodness of human hands: they flex and they are deserving.

But what have we taken or purchased that we have not used? Locke could likely not imagine a society as casually ornamental as ours, as dumbly acquisitory, purchasing for the sake of purchasing. That given a small bit of surplus we all pulse toward largesse, frivolity. But could he imagine buying something because it is beautiful or because it fills our hearts to breaking and then our hearts break and we call it home? Would he forgive owning land because strands of it furled down inside of us when we were just children, before we had any choice, though we wouldn't have chosen any differently? And even though we don't live there, will never live there, will only visit in short bursts every summer, we want to own it, all of it, and we want it to stay exactly the same.

My dad owns a large, undeveloped shore lot about a half mile up the river from the Benson family land where we spent our summers. He bought it cheaply years ago before people realized there was a finite amount of shore acreage left in the world. Due to recent wetlands protection acts, my dad now can't build the house he'd like to build on the lot — he's too late for everything, the curse of the cautious man. Unless they want to build a house on stilts or concrete blocks, I doubt that any buyers could do much more than put a trailer or a small cabin on the lot. So now he wants to sell it. But the thought of that ignites a fever of greed in me. I'll take over the taxes I can't afford, I'll apply for a loan for which I won't be considered, anything so it doesn't become someone else's. This land is my land; it is not also your land.

How can we trust ourselves with property when it can be had merely for money and desire? Why are these two together reason enough to be able to take something and do with it what we will? There are many things I've wanted and taken and have not used or have not used well. I'm sure we all have these things. Still, we trust ourselves to be better stewards (if we can even imagine ourselves merely stewards) than other people who may or may not, in fact, be more destructive than ourselves. I want that land. I don't want anyone else to have it. This is also how I have treated the sparkling-eyed boy, among others. I want to be able to leave, fill my stomach with pomegranate or abalone, my lungs with cologne or the carcinogenic fumes of buses; then come back and know my lot has been waiting, unchanged.

Property may be humankind's answer to our disillusionment with relationships — we find we can't own people, at least not literally, through love, slavery, or reproduction. Unshackled, people are so slippery. What else can we pin down? Animals, the great backs of rock, the spines of trees. And why is shopping so often the refuge of unhappy people, the handles of those crisp, portable bags curled in their palms? Why at twenty-nine and three years single did I buy a house I could barely afford in a town where I didn't intend to stay long?

How do we contain a parcel of land? How do we measure it and mark its boundaries? It seems like an abstract proposition, as impossible as turning this map in front of us into a swath of land that breathes through millions of tiny mouths we have chosen to call stomata (naming — another act of proprietorship). Individual parts of the land — needle, leaf, bud, stalk, pod, fruit — have their skins to contain them, to mark the end of themselves and the beginning of something else. But the scent of the forest, its rustlings, its moisture, sap, trickling streams, these things have no skin. Part of our forest is wafting north into Canada, part of it is dumping into the St. Mary's River, the St. Lawrence Seaway, the Indian Ocean.

Nonetheless, my father is having the Benson property surveyed. Animals piss or fight. Trees spread, prick, poison, or refuse to be digested. Rocks recline heavily into the ground. We have our own ways of marking property, utilitarian instincts acting extravagantly. Red sticks like a warning or enticement will be tamped in every eighth of a mile or so along the edge of our property, marking the end? the beginning? An age is over — I feel I'm learning the rules of ownership for the first time, and they seem bewildering, arbitrary. My great-grandfather bought this land for almost nothing (then and now) at the close of the nineteenth century. And yet we, by accident of birth, own just as soundly as the sparkling-eyed boy, who builds houses and barns and garages sixteen hours a day, six months a year, to buy his own land. And if I have children, they will own this land, too. And so on, for centuries, maybe. Astounding. Why do I feel like a child having to be told for the fourteenth time that the sky isn't really blue, it just looks that way?

There is no undoing these patterns, is there? Surely we need rules for ownership, and those of familial inheritance seem to be the only ones we can count on—allowing our progeny to dote on us at our deathbeds and then take what we can't take with us. But who is my father to tell me what I will own, who was his father, who will I be? And could something so primal as where we situate ourselves on the globe, what water we drink, what trees become the definition of *tree,* what temperatures we can stand, how we will treat the rest of the world for as long as we live, be determined by money, market, real estate? No. I think we should, at the very least, fight for our land and the elemental identity it brings along, fight and trail our intestines along behind us if we must, stain the ground we choose. We should fight not to conquer the land, but to be conquered by it.

This tepid map-making, this unintentional brushing of skin lightly on skin. I'm thinking that, instead, the sparkling-eyed boy and I should be rutting on our property line, the forest floor embedding itself in our hides, open maws threatening the insides of each other's bodies. But that is another matter entirely, a matter I can try to invent in his wife's eyes but that doesn't exist in his.

When my great-grandfather bought this land, he got about a half mile of shore along the St. Mary's River (a broad river five miles across that looks much more like a large lake) and a deeper, wider forest blooming behind it. He had a shadow wife and eight difficult children who never liked one another much. (I didn't realize when I was small that not all families were afflicted with such enmity.) When he died, he left each of his eight children a shore lot to do with what that child would. Three of his children, including my grandfather, built small summer cabins in the fifties. Two more eventually put trailers on their lots, and the rest never used their land. But what to do about the approximately ninety acres of woods rising from the shore? Rather than carve up the woods into inheritable parcels, he left the woods to his children and their children, and so on, collectively. None of us can sell our woods property. What would we sell? A random square in the cedar bog? A triangle by the Oberly Pass? We are all (who knows how many now) bound to each other through ownership, taxes, our agreement to barely tolerate one another.

My father long ago acquired one of the shore lots from a childless uncle, and on it we built our one-room cabin and a shower house. It's modest and rustic — it has no running water in the winter months, and he brought in the only phone line on the Benson land just a few years ago. No one, except now my father since he retired, lives on this property year-round. The road is too small, the snowfall too enthusiastic, the winter sun extracting light rather than shedding it. Even in the summer, when this particular slice of water and land are warmed to near perfection — or as near perfection as a blue-collar clan can hope to get — only a few Bensons visit, some for weekends from Detroit, some for the whole summer as we used to do and as my grandmother still does in her husband's cabin, at eighty-nine a hearty widow.

Since the loggers had gorged themselves in the last twenty years of the nineteenth century, nothing much was left for the next generation. Some of my great-grandfather's children scattered, jobless. My grandfather and a few others moved downstate when they came of age. The car industry in Detroit called like a siren they already knew was ugly and deadly but had to run after anyway. Those boys wilted, came home when they could. But the next generation, the generation of my father and his cousins, born into the thirties, the war, the birth of the suburbs — they couldn't find their way home as easily, a migratory pattern disturbed. My father, however, a Depression baby, a draftsman, felt exiled from this family land and never learned to sink into Detroit and take root. He perched, spending his every vacation and weekend as a young man on this land in the Upper Peninsula. He wouldn't even buy a house in the city — he spent the first ten years of his marriage in his parents' attic, imposing his exile on my mother as well. So he could spend the summer up north, he quit his non-union draftsman job every summer as soon as we were out of school and mildly hoped to get it back the next fall. He was born displaced and homesick, and he passed the sickness on to us.

My father, I think, has lost hope of my sister or me marrying, but I suspect he is secretly relieved, having told us many times about prenuptial agreements, as if we were the daughters of a Big Three executive rather than a draftsman. He's worried about his land, someone taking it from him — rather, from the idea of himself reflected imperfectly in us. I might take this worry of his as a lack of confidence in my ability to choose a suitable mate: if not a lasting one, at least a kind and decent one. But I saw my painfully kind mother give him almost everything she had worked for just to get free from the marriage — and still he was suspicious, like a scavenger choked with offal, sure she would come after his family land. What can we say for ourselves if we cannot say that we understand even slightly the person we have lived with for thirty-five years? Or, rather, if we must admit that we understand and still can't help our fears from rolling like lava over people we tried weakly to love.

But this is the point that I am grinding: we continue to trust in the sagacity of the human brain when we have such suffocating evidence to the contrary. We trust ourselves to own a thing that lives and breathes of its own accord. For some reason, we have not yet learned to fear ourselves enough — the great and terrible things we can do and our inability to tell the difference between them. Why this trust? Because we have such desires, such wood smoke, charred-cartilage-steeped desires, that we create elaborate and civilized-seeming systems such as property laws to disguise them. Thomas Hobbes described these instincts (the teeth, the claws), but he didn't acknowledge that *anything* could be borne of them, even his own *Leviathan*.

The road to our habitable shore, just a path, really, a trail, dead-ends into nearly impassable shore/forest that stretches for miles down the St. Mary's. We are the last humans for those same miles. The children of my great-grandfather, Wallace Benson, got together and put up a gate at the head of the path. I doubt it can actually swing shut anymore, but it hunkers there with a dark heart surging into signs — Keep Out, Private Property, and Posted: No Trespassing. What have we been guarding? What needs such protection? At the end of the dead-end road, we listened, suspicious of every stone popping under a wheel tire. "God damn it, can't they read the sign?" Our blood would rise to our skin at the occasional stray car that would roll down, turn around, and roll back. Or the tourist couple out for a walk, raising a hand at us in a wave. We'd freeze as if we were a different species, as if something about us might be stolen. We wanted privacy before the world was crowded. It is a national epidemic, the idea of the frontier ticking in the core of each American, wearing out the cage of our ribs.

How did we survive Detroit and the pageantry of its suburbs? My father built an eight-foot wooden fence around our modest back patio before he would have dinner there. With it, he taught us the irreparable narcissism: everyone wants to look at us, everyone has a judgment. Some people who believe this try to put on a show, others use space as a shield, perhaps even as a weapon. Some people do both.

A few days ago my father and I took a walk down the shore. This has never before been possible in my lifetime. In an apparently normal fluctuation, the water has retracted so that there is land where there wasn't land before. The new ground stretches like a leg after the cast has been removed—pale, damp, hairy with the stubble of reeds. But for a shore walk, we will take what we can get. And what we get is deer and fox at the edge of the trees, evidence of fish caught and mauled, and a bald eagle in its nest about a mile from our home. The eagles have chosen an old tree on Carlton Point—a spit of land that juts out about fifty yards from the shoreline. When we reach the point, my father tells me what he clearly has been worrying over for months, with stomachfuls of acid, sleepless nights. An unnamed corporate interest has acquired the point and a good bit of land beyond it—pure limestone and dolomite under the scalp of forest. They might mine it, as another company mined Lime Island across the bay, and still another today quarries Drummond Island, twenty miles down the river at the mouth of Lake Huron. If they build a quarry, there will be dynamite, cranes, bulldozers, cargo freighters, pulling up to the point, widening rainbows of fuel on the water, white powder settling over everything. They will open up our stunted road to daily, heavy, peering traffic.

He has rolled up the map, and his wife's face tells me it's time to go. Owning produces a crucible of our worst impulses: we would do anything to protect our interests—hurt, lie, steal, cheat—because they are ours. But there can also be great love, love that we seem to read along our bones, when we are wed to what we know is ours. We are ashamed to be in love with land, though, so we find other words for the relationship: ownership, proprietorship. Because we don't know how to love and then let go, we find other words for that, too. The sparkling-eyed boy is buying property, and though in my fears I want to seduce him, I would rather he stayed with his wife, raised children who will also stay and learn the difficult way to be owned by this land.

Souvenirs, Summer 2001

I can't wait to be submerged. Home again to where this one Great Lake is cold and impossibly clear. I have been an inconstant lover, leaving and returning sporadically. But the lake could never miss me the way I miss it. Besides the slight bit of heat it's drawing from my body, it is indifferent to me; whereas I try to embrace it over and over as I wade in. It drips from my puckered skin.

About seventy yards out, the water is well over my head. I look down at my body dangling under the surface in milky, translucent underwear. I can see my clothes in a dark pile on the empty beach. I haven't considered what I might do if someone comes along — someones so rarely do. My tiny car — its engine hot from the long drive, its trunk still full of my bags — is parked out of sight at the side of the two-lane highway next to a small green sign that says Great Lakes Circle Tour. But I feel as if this shore, this lake, must be my secret. Under me I can see the sand perfectly repeating the same ridge all the way to shore. The sun in the water looks tangible, shattering against the bottom and zagging everywhere. This is a show only the three of us could put on, sun and water and human eyes.

I will be thirty shortly. I have forty-five years left. Perhaps more, perhaps not nearly so many. That isn't a lot of time, really, and I have been courting the wrong beasts: water, sunlight, summer, married boys with sparkling eyes embedded with pieces of myself. Which of these could I squeeze in my lined palm until its breakable bones hurt? I want something that is mine, that stays.

This beach has always been here, hasn't it, its boulders on either end, soft sand stretched across its middle? At least, for an "always" I can imagine. This is the same beach where he carried me down to the water, cried into my jeans. Where my dog, who's now dead, left her fierce, running footprints; where my sister and I as girls dug tunnels in the sand until our hands met as our hands never meet now; where I walked back and forth every summer for seventeen years, dragging my toes in the sand, studying the line where water thins to damp nothing and land swells up into pebbles, then sand, then blade, then road, then tree to infinity; where stones have waited patiently on shore to be roughly stroked by waves into sand or to be plucked one by one for their greenness or their pinkness or their deep glitter or their fossilized creatures and taken home to dressers and gardens where, once dry, they will inevitably disappoint. Would I like to say I have learned to leave these stones behind? I am almost thirty. I know the drill. I will take a few with me when I leave.

People might find them in a box or a wooden bowl some day when the water has dried from my hair and the freckles retreated from my skin and my veins have collapsed and my hands no longer clench around the things I thought might save me. They might throw out my sweaters, receipts, old notebooks, but they might like the weight of these rocks in their hands, they might want to take them home.

Walking Diary, Summer 2001

DAY I

It's a mental defect, this nostalgia. I have a week to myself in the cabin while my father is in Russia on a trip. A week to write, to see my thirtieth birthday coming, to think about what matters.

What I notice first when I am here is that I feel immediately and precisely as if I am in love, heartbroken. But in love with, broken by what or whom? Honestly, I think I'm besotted with dirt and the things that spring up out of it and the places where it dissolves into water. Every day while I am here I take a long, embarrassingly vigorous walk down the road for maybe five miles, and everything I look at reminds me of some moment or mood — a violent lurch in the center of my gut that turns memory into a real emotion. Isn't that the meaning of nostalgia — to feel in the present an emotion that belongs to a different time? I'm not referring merely to emotions attached to other humans. I trip up at the sight of low hills tumbling down to the water and of stark contrasts — sky, islands, water, shore, woods — variations on green and blue with splashes of white, yellow, brown, thrown in with the near purple of the opposite shore. The air is saturated with light constantly shifting under the archipelagoes of clouds. Yes, just being here is like being in love — finding movingly beautiful what someone else might deem unremarkable. I fell for this gesture of land and water a long time ago, but the rest of my life is somewhere else, and a week at a time is not enough. Thus, it's only partly true that I am in love with the sparkling-eyed boy. Or, rather, if I love him it is a sorely conditional love: I cannot imagine loving him in any other place. To me, he *is* this undiscovered place. Outside of it, I would have to hold him up against others, and I'm afraid he would look very different.

Sure, I say this like a sage, as if love is a mere psychological tick that can be explained by a time and a place, by something that we want captured and preserved, by some need of ours to have an emotion we can't get on our own, to find someone whom we can carve ourselves all over. We can, no doubt, de-mystify our own love, yank its pretty clothes off and watch it freeze or burn. But on my walk today, I thought I saw him. On the side of a house not far from his own, a few men were getting ready to reshingle the roof. A flatbed truck piled with boxes of shingles (I remember those boxes, pulling sheets out and handing them to him, trying not to look as if I was straining). A man pulling himself lightly onto the truck from the ground. Something about the length of him, the straight width of his shoulders, the way the baseball cap sat on his head. I was sure this was the back of the sparkling-eyed boy. If I can demystify these feelings, why did I immediately tremble all over, want to melt into the ditch? Why is this imagined love more compelling than reality? It is not because the love would be more stunning. We would not have a glamorous life: he is not exceptionally beautiful, brilliant, or kind, and neither am I. He doesn't see the point of traveling; I would suffer and whine every year when our world froze over. But what does that logic have to do with my shaking hands, the constriction in my throat? That light leap of his reminds me of every moment deep in the past of this place.

I plot on my way to my turnaround spot and back to the shingleless house how, if he is still on the ground when I get there, I will call out his name, pretend that sweat isn't running into my eyes, and tell him I must talk to him. *Will you meet me? Don't worry, I just want to talk.* As if talk is the least dangerous thing we might do together instead of the most.

And what will I say to him? That I am nostalgic? Isn't that a pleasant story I tell myself—we can still love each other in some platonic, edifying way *and* have the lives that we've chosen? Will I tell him that I love this place despite my having forsaken it, him? I need him to tell me that it's okay, that I belong still, that this land has, he has, never left me. That there is constancy in the world, and despite my wavering I can have it. He has no idea how much ballast he might hold for me and yet how his easy leap makes me tremble like a lunatic. I approach the house (there is no way around it), trying not to examine it too obviously. One guy is ripping gutters from the front, another is setting up a ladder. But I don't see the man I thought was the sparkling-eyed boy anywhere. Thank god.

⊸

DAY 2

Today on my walk, I really did see him. Late afternoon on a Friday, I had already passed his house on the way up to the turnaround spot (where the two-lane highway begins) and was coming back when, a hundred yards or so in front of me, a green minivan appeared at the end of a driveway and slowly pulled onto the road, rolling away from me. Of course, it was his driveway and he was the driver. There before me was all of the evidence I could ever need of his adult life. A green minivan. Her choice, I'm sure—color, make, model. I could see the outline of her head above the passenger seat.

But I am more interested in hands, and arms, and what their movement might mean. He rolled to the end of the drive and looked in my direction, checking for traffic. How long did it take him to decide it was me, and what made him know? Perhaps something about my height, my build, the mechanics of my stride. I knew his back the day before (it was his back! they were working on that house!) almost immediately. But my eye had been waiting for signs of him, searching the cab of each pickup that passed for something familiar in the shape of the driver. Perhaps it was something less essential. My hair, short and blond, the same cut he had seen last year. Could he see my expression from there, frozen, as if I'd been caught doing something? (Was I not supposed to walk past his house?) Whatever it was that gave me away, he raised an arm out the window in the traditional, efficient, country way — no flourish of a wave at the end, just a hand in the air. But as the minivan pulled onto the road, I saw her hand go up, too, and flutter in the air. He must have said something to her.

Too much fuel for both of us women, sparkling-eyed boy. Better for you to have ignored me. My mind degenerated into a sludge of useless questions: Did he wave instinctively, merely acknowledging someone he knew? Did he weigh his options for a moment: can I just ignore her, will my wife mind if I wave? Did he wish he could have been alone in his pickup instead, turning toward me instead of away? He probably said, "I think that's Amy Benson down the road." Perhaps she had asked, "Who's that?" when he waved, and he answered, carefully uninterested, reluctant to share the private knowledge of my presence up there. Or, a private dread, he said, genuinely nonchalant: "That looks like Rich Benson's girl."

And what do I do in response to the wave? I lift my arm tentatively, as if they were coming toward me in the dark with their brightest lights on, though they'd turned the other way and it was broad daylight. And then, fool that I am, I start run-

ning. I start running because, up here, no one takes a walk on
the road for exercise or pleasure; it just isn't done. Most people
work for a living. They lift and stamp and pound and carry and
get home with a weariness they can taste in their mouths. So I
figure I'd look more purposeful, less ridiculous running instead
of swiftly walking. I didn't realize until after I noticed how
slowly the minivan was going once it hit the road that it must
have looked as if I'd started running after them.

You know, I have a good life. Friends, perhaps a hint of love
with a new fellow in New York, family, a job, good students, a
house, books, a brand of pen I love to use. What is this picture
doing in it? A green minivan rolling down the road, nuclear
family inside, and me, running after it.

❧

DAY 3

He is cruel. He has not come to see me. When I know he
knows I'm here, I begin the fruitless waiting.

Today on my walk, I barely even glanced toward his house.
When I got near, I resumed the charade of running and
dropped it again as I reached the woods on the other side and
was out of sight. I've always wanted to be a runner. Runners
seem so noble, disciplined, utilitarian in form, the nonessentials
burned away. But, walker that I am, my body does not admire it.
My lungs immediately burn and my hips ache. I do hope he ap-
preciates the things I have pretended for him and the very real
sweat that is splashing to the pavement. Maybe someday my
fierce independence, my discipline, will be real, as real as my
lack of interest will be when I don't look toward his house.

Though we have seen each other about four times now in as
many years, he has not sought me out since our adolescence,

so I don't know why I expect it now. I know he knows the way. He knows all of the roads up here. They have names but rarely signs: Gogomain, Prentiss Bay, Traynor, Four Lake, and Lime Island. I'm thinking of putting up big orange arrows that point the way right up to the cabin door. But that would be too obvious, I think, like the flaming butts of monkeys. I don't want to give the wrong impression.

Perhaps I should just trust in his sense memory. Every summer day, at first, before we accepted the requirements of encroaching adulthood, every day we met at the dock practically in front of our cabin. We were good beasts back then! Without ever touching, we made our bodies feel so good, dunked in cool water, divorced from the exactitudes of land.

The ice has long since cracked and gone under, daylight lingers, the forest is choked with new leaves, and there is a scent in the air rich with living things before they turn the sharp corner toward winter. Don't you remember what this means? Am I not part of the breaths to be drawn before the air once again freezes your lungs? My dear boy, come speak with me. Let us be good beasts together again.

DAY 4

Forever, poets have known what a strange thing it is to know we are dying long before we actually do. I keep walking, feeling parts of me quiver when my heels strike the pavement. I will never be firm all over, of a piece. How can we smile and feel satisfied when we know our cells get a day older every day, our minds less and less able to think a new thing or to hold a thought for long?

When I am honest, I must admit to believing sometimes that I am a sickness and he could hand me back well again. All I need to hear is a few words from him; that's all, words. There is the world whole and portentous; and then there is the world in shards, spent, discovered. How can we help ourselves from preferring the fantasy — the unbroken, benevolent world, high sun on the same perfectly shaped leaf multiplied, hanging everywhere. The earth really was blue and green, and we loved it as if it could love us back.

He is wise to stay away from me. We shouldn't say to one another everything that we could.

⤝

DAY 5

I didn't go on a walk today. I am relaxing into the deep nothingness of no expectations. I have been telling myself: There is nothing else that I want besides this moment on a wooden bench in front of the cabin, looking out onto the water, a velvety breeze blowing through the trees, across me. I am trying to feel merely like an object with planes and curves the air must negotiate. It doesn't count, though, if I have to tell myself this. I realize with consternation that I have almost no idea how to be without design or a wish formed for the next moment. Among a thousand other things, I have been tuned to hear the phone ring (which it does not do) or the crunch of tires on the gravel (which does not come). I like to think that, as an adult, I have barely walked across the street for a man, let alone waited for the phone to ring. But this is an old anticipation made new. We had no phone here when I was a kid, so the crunch of tires meant a possible visitor. As a teenager, my life was marred by waiting for someone to drive down the road and become an actor in my drama. I can't decide if it's crueler to have or not have these anticipations. I used to think satisfaction equaled stagnation, then a slow sinking into the muck. Either way, I am trying to release my desires as if they were a buildup of toxic fumes. Ah, but how sad! He might come when I no longer care if he comes. Rather, if he comes, I might necessarily no longer care. Are we all built for living only in our minds?

I don't know what the sparkling-eyed boy tells himself he'd really like to do if only he could. I don't know his heart anymore. Why shouldn't it change every day, like mine? Why shouldn't we fall into the distance between us and lose each other wholly? This is not the stuff of tragedies. But what fascinates me is that there are so many things we can know and so many things we can feel and how rarely those two lists intersect. If I have worked hard to solve the mystery of why I have dreams about him, to consciously understand my subconscious, then why do I still dream about him? Explanation can't quell a more powerful urge at work here: to be dissatisfied, to feel only loss is worthy of courtship. To hell with our better judgment—there is no such thing when we don't really want to listen to it.

God help the perpetually bereft—and who among us is not one of those? Don't come to me, sparkling-eyed boy. I couldn't take the satisfaction.

❧

DAY 6

After two days of rain, I am walking again. There is a chill in the air at eleven in the morning, and I am walking only for myself, knowing that I will not see him and he will not come.

I am stumped. I have decided my life can't be about absence, what I don't have, what does not abide, and the rich grief it brings. "Life Is Elsewhere" was the easy slogan of young,

French students. In me, its bittersweet grows more bitter.

But if I am not an absence, I'm terrified to ask, what is my substance? The trees are defined by the texture of their bark, the cluster of their leaves or needles, how they make their genes known to the world, whether or not they fall to pieces come October. The animals are divided by the temperature of their blood, how they hide their entrails, the solidity of their bones, and the splay of those bones inside their skins. But each of us? How are we to differentiate the blank complexity of our consciousness? I cannot say what I am from moment to moment. One moment I am a perception, the next an idea, the next a limbic fear.

I have had one overwhelming thought about the sparkling-eyed boy: that he would be able to tell me something I have desperately needed to know. I thought he might have kept something essential about who I was safe and unaltered. And I could add that essential something to who I am now and know myself better. Frankly, I have been wanting a mirror, and have wanted to be a mirror for him. But I think we must answer these unanswerable questions for ourselves. Here, though, I reach the kernel of my cowardice. I fear my own volition. I am afraid to be alone with myself. And I am not, I imagine, alone in this. We call it loneliness because loneliness is an acceptable emotion. But this fear is much stranger and inviolate — it is the fear of being in charge of a whole person and having no idea how to govern it or what *it* even is. What we are and the soundness of our choices are nearly wholly unverifiable.

I wish I felt more like an animal: working blood and air through my body, moving along the edge of trees and water, a collection of jerking, purposeful limbs. But I still look into the darkness of the forest where trees have uninvited light, and I am afraid. I need to stay on the road, a path not of my own making. I need to know other humans have walked here and have found it good. I need, apparently, not to know what I am and how I will fill my days.

❧

DAY 7

There it is, like an icy vein flowing out of the ground — or the fingers of a dead thing refusing to concede — or, rather, something so pure it doesn't know it should stay covered. Five almost-translucent pearly stems pushing out of the black dirt in the shadiest part of the woods, long necks curved over tightly like swans, a shy head the same color tucked below it. These are not flowers or absurdly headed moss; they are Indian ghost pipes, a fungus, and they bend their heads away from one another in a small circle as if they are guarding something necessary inside. Maybe I love things best that no one metaphor can describe, no single chapter can explain.

I could have easily missed this. Today I took a woods hike instead of a walk. It's been a long time since I've been in the woods alone, so I missed the trail marker early on and plunged, instead, into uncharted land. I was fine for a while, but then, when I didn't find the trail I told myself I wasn't looking for, a kind of low-grade panic set in. A purely instinctual panic, wholly divorced from my intellect, which told me I couldn't really get lost. All I would need to do is head downhill and eventually I'd hit the shore. I started to stumble — the trees were closer and closer together, a few sharp branches beading up blood on my arms. But then I saw the Indian pipes like a bit of lightning from the ground, and, moments after I left them, I reconnected with the path.

My destination was an abandoned homestead about two miles in. A long time ago a man named Jimmy Moore used to live there without a single other person, without a road even. Just Jimmy and the trees. He had cleared a large meadow (smaller now every year), and you can still see his stone well and the foundation of his house. Apparently he hiked out once in a while to get supplies, but he stopped coming one year. People say he just disappeared, since his body was never found.

So in the middle of a large stretch of woods unbroken by roads, I am alone with the traces of a man no one really knew. I sit at the edge of his old well and try to think about what this means, but I am antsy, the flies are biting. I never learned the art of meditation. I need to turn back to my father's cabin at the edge of the woods, closer, at least, to people I love. It's good to know how thoroughly I'm incapable of Jimmy Moore's misanthropy or courage. Was he filled with weakness or hope, and which one am I full of?

Let's call it hope. I'm tired of accusing myself. We have so little time conscious here on our plot of earth, in the heat of its colors. And, truly, this place has us — you, the sparkling-eyed boy, me — for just a little time. There are many ways to be here but not here. Jimmy Moore's place and the sparkling-eyed boy are reliquaries. I tell stories about them, visit them to point out fragments from the past. They become indelible legends. The ghost pipes, though, are elusive, off the trail, gifts appearing for the sake of themselves. How easily I could never have seen them — it's much easier to find a dried-up well. It's much easier to fixate on a tangible person than a certain sweet scent in the air you can find nowhere else, or the way light shifts on water so beautifully you find it difficult to breathe.

I am gliding through the forest in my own ghostliness. I want to hang on to the meanings that rise and fall away in a heartbeat. But a place is not about my use of it. A place simply is, regardless of the stories we'll stitch to it. Here is my hope: that one day I won't hurry back from where I go. For a moment as fleeting as a metaphor, I will pause and be amazed and breathe as I've never breathed before, through new, dying lungs.

⊷

NIGHT 8

Sometimes I think, you say. *Sometimes I think,* you say. We are red with the heat of our bodies, white in the center, orange like steam off our skin, the evaporation of yellow to green, to deep blue beyond the porch light, to the deep cold of indigo farther into the night, the core of an iceberg. *Sometimes I think,* you say. The sun has gone down and you have come down and the world has gone so dark we could be anywhere. We could take a step sideways and fall off. We could end up two bright spots in the core of a glacier melting very little. My father is a crimson core at the end of the driveway who refuses to go away. He is afraid of our skin and the words that might loosen themselves from the tiny spaces between our teeth. *Sometimes I think,* you say, *I will go crazy in a couple of years.* And any ears could hear you, standing near you as we are. My father's ears and mine and birds still awake to hear our peculiar chattering. The insects love us and are frantic for our hides. I slap at myself as if annoyed with my elbow, neck, shin. You move your big hand in a thoughtful wave. The road has been there the whole time, from the beginning to the end. Only this night you came down it, your truck a violence passing between trees. You say, *Sometimes I think ten years have gone by, ten years have gone by, ten years.* Ten years — count back ten to when you got married, when you said those things you hoped to mean always. Thirteen years to when I kissed you in your truck, when your hand held the ends of a clump of my hair, the underside of a small breast. Do you see how the light falls around us and at its edge the dark rises, confident and complete? This moment could be that moment or the ones before that. But your hands look rough and swollen now, my forehead deeply creased, my thighs ticked with dark little vessels. You say, *Sometimes I think ten years have gone by and I have nothing to show for it.* I say, *What about your beautiful little girl?* I say but don't say, I have pictures of your deep reservoirs of joy. Have you given them all to her, distilled? Have you kept a vial of the impurities for yourself: sadness, frustration, resignation? I say but don't say, Though I have been sadder, it makes me very sad to know you are so sad. I say but don't say, I hope this means that you miss me. The mosquitoes are leaving drams of poison under our skin. I have asked but not asked my father to leave us. He doesn't understand what is happening, but neither do we. Warm things are almost never elemental. Elemental things do not speak—as if vibrating air through our throats to change our lives or the lives of others could ever be the business of a rock. I have never wanted to be a person occupying a body on a particular square of earth at a particular time, but here I am, unable to negotiate the hereness of us.

Start at the beginning: We are at the edge of pine trees, the edge of the water. I have known this spot since I was born; you have known it with me. We are not the most significant clusters of particles. Not even close. We are warm spots in a cooling night, a cooling season, cooling lives. Deep in our forest there is a four-billion-year-old stone ridge. Scientists can tell us these things. My father, a bewildered core at the end of the driveway, is proud of this ridge. I am terrified by it. I think you might be sadder than me. I am terrified by that, too. You say, *Sometimes I think,* you say, *there is so much to worry about now. Things were better in high school. We only had to decide where the party was going to be on the weekends.* You laugh, a sound like silt in your throat. You don't know, do you, how few of us are capable of your grins. I say but don't say, Do you know what you want to return to, what you would have to seal up and bury? I say, *Yeah, it's hard to let that stuff go, isn't it.* As if I am a former addict and you an addict.

But we are both slapping our bodies, the insects on our bodies. We both wish we could step backwards out of the circle of light, leaving the frightened rouge core of my father, every inch articulated. In the field behind the cabin, the blind indigo field, we would become indistinct from the field except for the red glow of our human heat. Without even seeing my face, my hand slapping blindly at my skin, you could say what you've said but not said. I could say what I've said but not said.

Have I gotten that right? That you haven't said all you would say? You say, *Sometimes I think I will go crazy.* But you are a warm spot and the rest of the night is blue-black and cold. I ask but do not ask, What about the other times — what do you think then?

↬

DAY 9

I began with a central question: Why? Why did the sparkling-eyed boy visit my dreams unpredictably but often, the same scenario every time telling me I *still* wasn't satisfied? After years of forgetting him, why when I saw the video of his wedding did my heart stumble, my lungs freeze? This is a mystery story, and I keep writing it because I'm never convinced I've figured it out. We are not tightly woven, plot-driven novels. We are all just small collections of events, impressions, moods, beliefs, which, in shards, we call our selves. Hold the shards up to the light, give them a twist, and you will have a kaleidoscope: a sharp-petaled flower, next an angry snowflake, next a shapeless spill of ink.

I am tempted to say, Aha! That is my problem: I have been looking shard by shard, but stand back and I will have the whole, fluid mosaic. But I'm afraid there is no perspective from which we can view every angle of a moment, let alone a year, a life, or the life of another. And there is no answer if I have to answer the question myself.

He came last night, driving too fast down our road. An hour earlier, my father and I had stopped at his house on the way back from the beach. I didn't ask him to, didn't mention the boy at all; my dad wanted to pay the sparkling-eyed boy for reshingling the roof of the cabin. He was on a tractor mower, holding his little girl in front of him. She marched right up to me, took my hand, and dragged me from spot to spot in front of the house while my father talked with him and his wife. The girl squealed and laughed and threw herself on the ground with a hilarity a body many times her size couldn't contain. The sparkling-eyed boy asked me about my job, he remembered that I write. When we left, the rosy girl said, *Where are you going?* She said, *No! Don't go.* He said, *You should come back this week, take her to the beach.* I said, *I'm leaving tomorrow morning.* Fifteen minutes after we got back he called — he just remembered that he never checked my dad's driveway for nails.

We all want something from one another. Perhaps someday this truth will not be so ugly to me as it is now, but it still seems like a poison, surreptitious and deadly. At the beginning, I wanted just this one love to be interest-free. I didn't want love to be merely what I give in order to get what I need — a primal bargaining chip. I wanted to remember him, let him know that he was precious, not leave my fingerprints all over him. I wanted a true gift to be possible: a gift to him and not myself.

I used to think that acceptance of ugly truths was acquiescence, was the providence of the old softening into their lives, apples browning inside their skins. I thought that feelings, ideals, meant something only if they were held forever. Was I wrong? With this book I am growing up. He was my childhood, a deeply rooted evergreen. He was the child I couldn't be and didn't have enough sense at the time to admire. But, in the strictest sense, what he is is all he has, what I am is all I have. And what I am is not wise enough to truly learn. Sentimental, but often secretly exacting. A martyr, acting as if I can bear what others cannot. Ruled by fear and not curiosity or logic or love. I am sometimes sad.

But not one single thing can refurl itself. Not a bud, not a fetus, not a firecracker, a sunrise, a wave, a volcano, a sentence. So here I am, unfurled, trying to be glad that seasons collapse in on themselves and living things die.

BREAD LOAF AND THE BAKELESS PRIZES

The Katharine Bakeless Nason Literary Publication Prizes were established in 1995 to expand Bread Loaf Writers' Conference's commitment to the support of emerging writers. Endowed by the LZ Francis Foundation, the prizes commemorate Middlebury College patron Katharine Bakeless Nason and launch the publication career of a poet, fiction writer, and creative nonfiction writer annually. Winning manuscripts are chosen in an open national competition by a distinguished judge in each genre. Winners are published by Houghton Mifflin Company in Mariner paperback original.

2003 JUDGES

Louise Glück, poetry

Jay Parini, fiction

Ted Conover, creative nonfiction